TRAINING
THE

Hunting Retriever

THE NEW PROGRAM

TRAINING
THE

Hunting Retriever

THE NEW PROGRAM

BILL TARRANT

Photographs by Bill Tarrant
with special credit to
Bill Berlat and Butch Goodwin

Foreword by Omar Driskill

HOWELL BOOK HOUSE

MACMILLAN • USA

To Sharon Tarrant Treaster
and her family:
Arden, Chad, Jeff
Terry and especially
Matt

Macmillan General Reference
A Simon & Schuster Macmillan Company
1633 Broadway
New York, NY 10019-6785

Macmillan Publishing Company is part of the Maxwell Communication Group of Companies.

Portions of this book first appeared in slightly different form in *Field & Stream,* copyright © 1983, 1984, 1985, 1986, 1987 by CBS Publications, the Consumer Publishing Division of CBS, Inc.; and in *Field & Stream,* copyright © 1988, 1989, 1990, 1991 by Times Mirror Magazines, Inc.

Library of Congress Cataloging-in-Publication Data
Tarrant, Bill.
    Training the hunting retriever/Bill Tarrant: photographs by
Bill Tarrant with special credit to Bill Berlat and Butch Goodwin.
        p.   cm.
    ISBN 0-87605-575-7
    1. Retrievers—Training.   I. Title.
  SF429.R4T38   1991   91-9343
  636.7'52—dc20   CIP

10   9
Printed in the United States of America

Contents

Foreword   vii

Introduction   ix

1. Picking Your Pup   1

2. Deserving the Pup You Picked   17

3. Yard Training   37

4. Fetching the Dummy   58

5. Water   88

6. The Magic Table   111

7. The Blind Retrieve   126

8. The Water Blind   137

9. The Looking Glass Drill   151

10. Pup and the Gun   161

11. A Bird in Hand   169

12. Early Bird Hunts   185

13. China Bird   189

14.   Waterfowl   195

15.   Popcorn Quail   208

16.   The Hunting Retriever Clubs   213

Appendix: First Aid for Water Dogs   215

Foreword

FROM 1930 TO 1980 the classic retriever trial circuit in America gradually slipped away from its reason for being. It no longer duplicated a day's hunt afield in its tests, goals or philosophy. It just became impossible for a bona fide waterfowl or upland bird hunter to test his hunting retriever in open competition with its peers. The retrievers running in the classic field trial circuit had to perform very difficult tests that demanded they trip over their own instincts, and when they didn't deny their own inner nature, they were forced into performing.

This was not for the true hunter or his retriever. There had to be another way. Then into this breach stepped Bill Tarrant. For years he had stood up to the nation telling them they were doing wrong, decrying the unnecessary pressure inflicted upon retrievers competing in the classic circuit, and pointing out for true conservation (for developing a retriever that could bring every bird shot to hand) that there had to be a new training and testing format.

Finally, in the April 1983 issue of *Field & Stream*, Bill's ink was replaced with fire. The nation was blasted with an immortal article, "The Mechanical Dog." Now every outdoor magazine's dog editor jumped on the bandwagon. A national clamor among the press was begun, and the bona fide bird hunters rallied in support of a program that placed emphasis on a retriever's natural instincts and innate hunting sense, which is superior to that of man in a bird field. They demanded, too, that the dog should have latitude in judgment while hunting and not be subservient to the will of man; in other words, not be mechanical in its actions.

Thus it came to pass that I was hunt marshal for the first hunting retriever test hunt ever conducted in the United States. I asked Bill Tarrant to judge. There could have been no one else.

Since then Bill has gone on and developed a complete training system for the hunting retriever trainer and has perfected the standard for what a true hunting retriever really is. Bill's training program is presented in this book.

There's just one other thing for me to mention in this Foreword. Tarrant's journalistic crusade broke through to success just as an eight-year crisis began in Canada bringing the worst drought our waterfowl resources have ever known since records have been kept. Tarrant's message was a godsend. Hunters had to bring to hand the few waterfowl they shot. Not a bird could be wasted. And the way to do that was with a trained hunting retriever.

Bill pioneered the biggest change to take place in retrievers in the twentieth century . . . and it took place at a critical time. It took place at the right time.

We now have dogs out there that hunt to the gun, dogs that track and trail cripples, tail-waggin' dogs that want to be out there saving ducks left and right. The goals are back: to help every hunter bring his retriever forward to the level of a savvy bona fide hunting dog.

Bill gave us our motto, "Conceived by hunters for hunters," when he wrote about those of us in muddy camouflage, running our dogs out of duck blinds, shooting our guns and testing just the way it was done in the field. The nation's hunters came back. Now there are well over 100 hunting retriever clubs that are making Bill's dreams a reality.

So it is a real pleasure for me to write the foreword to this book, *Training the Hunting Retriever*. The old-fashioned hunters and the old games they played went astray with their dogs, but the new hunting retriever was reborn because of the crusade of Bill Tarrant. If ever there is a hall of fame for gun dog enthusiasts, Bill Tarrant will truly be at the top.

The duck and upland game hunters of America say to the godfather of the new hunting retriever movement, "Bill, we love you."

Omar Driskill,
Founding President,
Hunting Retriever Club

Introduction

THE NEW hunting retriever movement has to be the most exciting thing that ever happened to the American waterfowl and upland game hunter. For not until now has there been a systematic, sensible, field-tested training program designed to produce a bona fide retriever gun dog. I don't just mean as a fetcher. I mean as a hunter of pheasant row crops, grouse tangles, quail coverts, duck blinds and goose pits. We're talking about a do-it-all dog that wears mud and cockleburs like rally stripes!

Secondary to actual hunting accomplishment, the bird hunter and retriever now have hunting retriever clubs to go to train, to learn, to develop and to crown their joint efforts with the dog earning the title Hunting Retriever Champion or even Grand Hunting Retriever Champion—and the hunter and dog alike wearing grins to last them the rest of their lives.

To put what I say in perspective, let's look at the history of the retriever in America. Though this book is written for the Labrador Retriever, Golden Retriever, Chesapeake Bay Retriever, Flat-Coated Retriever, Curly-Coated Retriever, Irish Water Spaniel, American Water Spaniel and any dog that will fetch, still the top dog in American and British history has been the Lab. So let's consider his fate. It mirrors all the rest.

The Lab was imported into America around 1930, by the blue-chip set on Long Island. These industrial and retail barons wanted a dog to fetch their ducks and dig out their pheasants. But not actually knowing how to train or handle a retriever, they often hired the professional trainer to come along with the dog. The result was the imported gamekeeper, who became the hands-on man in the dog's life. For the gentry were prone to say, "Well, we don't ride our racehorses, we let a proper jockey do that . . . neither should we be out kicking around the bush or having some dog leap up on our togs."

It wasn't years, but months, before these men (and women) were no longer satisfied with just watching their dogs do field work. The competitive character of these people goaded them into vying one dog against another. Thus the early birth of retriever field trials. Now, remember, the owners were not the handlers, so pity the poor dog trainer. To lose one weekend, that's accepted, twice, that's irritating, three times and that's preposterous. Winning was everything. So the dog trainer had to bear down to gain ever more miraculous feats from his charges. Until the field trial game disintegrated into a series of circus feats performed by mechanical dogs that were beaten, kicked, shocked, burned, shot and stomped to pass tests that demanded the dogs ignore their own instincts.

In other words, America developed a nonhunting Lab, or a canine robot.

Such nonsense is incomprehensible, but that's exactly what we did. And what happened then to the poor hunter with the flap-fendered pickup and bib overalls and mud-stained cuffs who owned and hunted a Lab? He became a second-class sportsman. For his dogs couldn't perform the circus tricks. All his dog could do was hunt and fetch. Can you imagine the lunacy of it all? The hunter and his Lab were acting out God's plan, but the field trial set was hell-bent on Man's plan, and the retrievers were brutalized and destroyed.

For who would want a pup out of a dog whose primary merit was its ability to handle high-voltage, low-amperage electricity, a heavy boot in the butt, a slingshot marble, a BB in the flank or a loaded whip across its chest? For the dog was treated this way to do the following: to swim senseless channel blinds and never touch land, while any hunting retriever would run down the shore, leap in and fetch up the duck; to pinpoint fallen birds without ever having to use his nose to scent for them, for his eyes were to be his major asset. Nonsense! A dog's eyesight is far from its keenest sense. Its nose, however, is uncanny. And now man has asked the dog to substitute its eyes for its nose! Incredible.

And what else happened? Well, no longer was the handler permitted to shoot game. That was to be done by official gunners. In real life does that mean the hunter was to throw rocks at the birds, or as I have written elsewhere, go on food stamps? And the field trial handler was obligated to wear a white coat so the dog could more easily detect hand signals. Ever go to a duck blind wearing a white coat? Get any ducks?

The stupidity went on and on. All the while the bona fide bird hunter with the gun dog Lab was being ridiculed by the gentry. But what's the real purpose of field trials (or as we call them here, test hunts)? It is to improve the breed. The winners are sought out to produce tomorrow's stellar performers. And what's the purpose of a test hunt: to duplicate a day's hunt afield! That's all! It's not to see if a dog can be forced to lay aside ten million years of instinct and break to man's whim.

So now we get to this book. Here the hunter is heralded. Here his hunting retriever is exalted. And more important: Here is where both hunter and dog are trained.

Here you'll learn the secrets, shortcuts and success of a hunting retriever trainer who's been in the business for thirty years. Where the approach will be to enhance the dog's innate abilities, not suppress them; where we will train with intimacy, not intimidation; where the ultimate goal is a great day afield, not beating a fellow hunter and his dog in competition; where God's plan is honored for man and dog alike, and the bird is brought to hand.

Getting started begins on the next page.

1

Picking Your Pup

BOYD HAMILTON of Sedona, Arizona, who calls himself retired oil-field trash, is a fishing buddy and helpmate of mine. I pick up a shovel and out of nowhere Boyd appears to pick up a rake. Boyd has a favorite expression he uses nearly every day. He'll say of unexpected opportunity, "Why, that's just like finding a bird's nest on the ground." What cat could be so lucky?

Well, there's no bird's nest on the ground when it comes to picking your pup. Matter of fact, odds of getting a great one are probably one in a million, so I decided long ago to spend my time prayin' instead of pickin'. It's like all pups ought to be named Lottery.

But there are some things to look for—things you probably never imagined and you certainly didn't read about in any other book—that we will reveal here.

For years I've talked of functional conformation. By that I mean I don't care what the dog looks like, I want to know if his physique and psyche can carry out the function of hunting a day afield. Another term for it, I guess, would be "genetic engineering." Or put more simply, "Is the dog an athlete and not a showpiece!" That's the point. Can he run, jump and swim, and do it with all his wits about him, not just running amuck.

Well, the way to get such a pup is to select him from such parents. That's why I never look at a pedigree. I look at the folks. I ask to see them hunt, I want to see them over birds, I want to see them in brush tangles and ice floes and muck to their shoulders.

I want to see them stand below the gun, to deliver the bird with a tender mouth, to leap about and position themselves for the next cast even if there's not been another shot. In other words, I'm looking for two necessities: the physique to do the job and the disposition to enjoy getting it done.

So what I'm doing at the kennel is looking at the parents, not the litter. When you've picked the sire and dam you think can get the job done, then just reach down, grab a pup and go. That's why it pays to study retrievers afield, learn of their mating, then call the breeder and tell him or her to select a pup and send it. You don't have to go to the kennel to get a great performer. You did your homework by studying the parents.

But all parents don't throw true. Some are prepotent (that is, they put their stamp on the get) and others throw unpredictably. And I've seen the oddity where the first generation didn't have what mom and dad had, but a second-tier mating of grandchildren threw back to the initial excellence of the first-generation parents. It's all a mystery. And thus you get the endless discussion: What's more important, the sire or the dam?

Well, most people will say the sire. For it's usually males that win the big trials or test hunts. Females are handicapped by coming into season twice a year and just don't have the equal opportunity to display their wares (bitches in heat can't be on field trial grounds). But I disagree. The bitch carries those puppies within her for sixty-three days, and we know there is cross-placenta behavior modification. Then she has the pups in the litter for seven weeks before you pick them up. So the bitch has had sixteen weeks to put her imprint on the pups—*and she does!*

A gun-shy bitch will throw gun-shy pups, hardmouth begets hardmouth, spookiness washes over the litter as well, just as boldness does or aggressiveness or grit. It goes on and on. But the dad—he's a traveling man. He spent his seed and left. His only influence is the genes he left behind. He wasn't there to modify behavior.

Bob Wehle, the world-famous English Pointer breeder who produces 150 pups a year, does not agree with me. He says in that hushed voice of his, "You see all matings don't nick [a word that means the mix produces something special]. You'll hear people say, 'Well, the bitch is more important than the male.' I just don't believe that. I believe that there are important female lines and there are important male lines. And I think this is well demonstrated in other breeding . . . in Holstein cattle for instance. You can trace families . . . where the female prevails. Now those females in that strong family will reproduce and they are probably a lot more important than the males they are being bred to.

"But by the same token there are male lines like those of Bold Ruler in thoroughbred horses. His sire produced, he produced, his son produced. It was a strong male line. So breed one of those horses to a mare and you get a dominant male line. And there I would say the male is more important.''

Then Wehle asks, ''Have you ever heard the term 'blue hen'? A blue hen is a thoroughbred term, and a blue hen is a mare that has produced a multitude of winners. No matter who you breed her to, she produces great horses. Well, I've been using the term for thirty years. Because in my lifetime I've probably had five blue hens in dogs. I could breed them to a fence post and get good pups, really. It made no difference who I bred to, they had great puppies. And every once in a while you run into a blue hen.''

Then Wehle takes another bent and explains, ''A lot of people don't understand about breeding any animal . . . about what I call the drag of the race. You can call it whatever you want. It's a tendency toward mediocrity. It's a fact that if you take five dogs, either of the same breed or of five different breeds, and you put them on an island and let them breed promiscuously, it would only be a question of time before the offspring would revert back to a common dog—probably to a wolflike nature. The color would be wolflike and all that.

''And I don't care what you start with, that will happen. In other words, the nature of things denies excellence. Because there's always this drag of the race. It's always withering away; no matter how far you proceed, you lose something each time you gain.

''So it's not good enough to breed to a mediocre dog. You have to breed to a dog that's extra special. He must have all the natural attributes, which is tenacity, the desire to find game, the ability to point, the ability to scent game at distances. But what separates dogs, from my point of view, is their intelligence.

''And I can separate the intelligent pups from those that are not at a very early age. If you just spend enough time with them and watch them . . . you can see the most precocious pups. Just simple little things. Some pups always know how to go through a gate, some pups can never figure it out. That's intelligence.

''So you subconsciously gravitate to the more intelligent dog and the dogs that have the personality that pleases you. And if you continue to breed that sort of a dog, that's what you'll end up with. Then performance is pretty much man-made from that time on . . . if you've got a dog with natural attributes and the intelligence and disposition, then you've got the perfect shooting dog . . . because you make him the perfect shooting dog.''

So there you have it. Two opposing points of view from Wehle and myself, two men who have spent a lifetime afield with sporting dogs. Take your pick.

Now to functional confirmation.

FUNCTIONAL CONFORMATION

At 10,000 feet we're Rocky Mountain high when dawn tips up cantaloupe-orange. We carry six Pointers and three Labs to this sheer, drop-off country to hunt blue grouse. Power performer in the pack is Web, the miracle Lab. He's been trained by professional trainer Mike Gould of Carbondale, Colorado, who seeks the ultimate hunting retriever.

Gould, the slightly built, dark-haired gun dog wizard, tells me, "You get a lot of Labs that can swim good, but they're not built right to run [what follows applies to all retriever breeds, as it will throughout this book]. A hunter needs a Lab that can hunt with the Pointers, can run wide and long and last all day.

"Before hunting season opened during August and the first week of September," Gould reveals, "we used Web for a strike dog. He'd locate the blue grouse, I'd whistle him to sit, then we'd check-cord our Pointer pups into the covey to steady them on birds. Remarkably, we had 727 grouse contacts, for I kept count. And with all the season dogs we brought up here, as well as the puppies—all the spaniels, Pointers, setters and retrievers, Web found 75 percent of the birds."

Web represents the essence of this book. Traditionally, retrievers have been walk-at-side or sit-at-side dogs waiting to be sent for the fetch of a bird some other dog pointed and/or flushed. No more. Now the retriever is our do-it-all dog: hunter, flusher, tracker and retriever. Gaining such versatile performance is what this book is all about. We're training *hunting retrievers*. Not only for excellence on a day's hunt but also as a contender in the new hunting retriever test-hunt format (more about this later).

I first met Web when he was one year old. Gould would cast him into a pond and he'd swim fifteen feet from shore while we walked a mile. Never once did Web seek the bank. He's the most biddable (and the birdiest) gun dog Lab I've ever met. His feats during the past five years have become legend. Not at field trials or test hunts, but out hunting wild birds.

Gould says, "Years ago I decided to work into a breeding pro-

The Labrador Web represents the essence of this book. Here he's shown with keenness and intensity beside author, gun and blue grouse. *Bill Berlat*

gram where I could acquire a dog that I consider to be a prototype, or a vision, of what I feel to be the most efficient Lab so far as running goes. The reason? In this up and down mountain country, if the Lab covers all the likely objectives, then I only need to walk to his finds. It saves the hunter.

"For a Lab to heel or quarter means the hunter duplicates all the dog's tracks. Let the Lab cast 100 to 250 yards out; up the mountain, down the canyon, out through thick brush, away yonder in that sea of alpine grass. The experienced handler can read his dog, know when he's making game, then whistle him down and go in to take his shots. That's why we call them hunters, isn't it? They do the hunting. We're the gunners."

I recall the years I released Labs in bobwhite fields only to call them off: They vacuumed the place clean.

Gould continues, "I studied every aspect of the Lab when I finally considered static and kinetic balance. From that I noticed that you needed a taller dog to achieve kinetic balance so he could sustain a race. The short-legged, heavyset dog just can't do it. Then everything else fell into place."

FEET

Mike Gould understands how and why every part of a good retriever matters. He goes on, "The feet are important. I studied the difference between a hare foot and a cat foot, and I learned with a hare-type foot you can get all kinds of speed out of the hole, but it's too tiring in a day's run. So you need a cat-type foot since it holds tight and gives the dog the endurance he needs."

FOREARM

"Also the length of the forearm is important. Like a horse. You want a horse that has a real nice slope to its pastern so the fetlock almost touches the ground when he moves. That gives him a shock absorber. It gives him the ability to absorb the jolt; especially in the front. And the dogs must have that same angle. If they're just straight up and down in the front legs, then it's too much shock. A postlegged dog by the second morning is so sore he can't hardly run because he's taken so much of a pounding in his shoulder."

Gould displays Web where "...everything fell into place."

TOENAILS

"But at the same time you don't want a sloping pastern with a big, long foot. You want a shorter foot with high toenails, so the nails won't strike rock and break off. A hanging nail can be a major irritant for a dog on a day's hunt."

LENGTH OF LEG

"Now, if you have a short-legged dog in the front, you end up with a chopped gait that sores the dog up in the elbows and the front end. Short legs in the back cause a rolling motion that makes the dog bounce when he runs: looks like he's stubbing his toes."

GREAT HEART GIRTH

Gould left this part out so I am sticking it in. A hunting retriever must have a great sprung rib cage with lots of flexibility. This trait gives him a life pump and an air conditioner. Let me explain. A pigeon-breasted dog will be running along and his heart and lungs will expand, but the ribs hold tight because of lack of spring. Well, that denies the dog oxygen, so he quits. Some hunter may charge the dog with having no spirit since he wouldn't sustain his race. But, heck, what happened is that the dog stopped to keep from having a stroke.

Also, the dog's nose is directly affected by the rib cage. A dog can only smell birds on the intake, never the outgo. If he runs through a narrow scent cone and the rib cage has closed down and the dog is now breathing in gasps, then of course he can't detect the bird's effluvium. But let the air conditioner of the rib cage be productive, and the dog can take long breaths even when he's hot and he'll detect that narrow scent cone when he races through.

ENDURANCE

Now back to Gould, saying, "I have a rule that I use: It's the third hour of the first day's hunt and the first hour of the third day's hunt that tells what kind of Lab you have before you. And in three hours most Labs in the country are dead in their tracks. But I'm building a Lab for the serious hunter. I'm talking about the Olympic Lab."

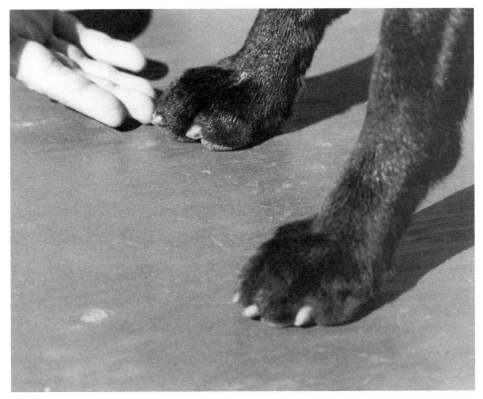

High toenails are less apt to break off and cost you the next day's hunt because of Pup's lameness.

Gould's in the field on birds—either hunting or training—most every day. His demand on Labs goes far beyond that of the casual hunter. Still, who wouldn't want an Olympic runner getting his bird-hunting message across, instead of a potlicker?

EXTENDED RANGE

Mike Gould continues, "The last thing I want to do when I'm out hunting is to tell a dog how to hunt. Web knows birds, he knows what we're doing, he knows he has permission to go out there and hunt. Now, I get a lot of complaints from other trainers about my emphasis on extended range. Last year I went hunting with a guy who had a real well-schooled spaniel. She had great quartering style, minded perfectly, sat at flush. The whole day out hunting with Web, this dog minded perfectly, looked great, very stylish, a beautiful dog, and the owner was happy as a lark. My dog was hunting all day . . . he appeared to be wild. To most people he would have looked like he was out of control.

"So on the way home this friend started ribbing me about Web. And I turned to him and said, 'How many birds did we shoot today?' He answered, 'We shot five.' I asked, 'How many did we shoot over Web?' 'Four,' came the answer. 'How many did we shoot over the other dogs?' 'We shot one over Web's son,' he said. 'How many did we shoot over the dog that minded perfectly?' 'Zero,' he had to admit, for the dog didn't get a bird up. So I said, 'What did we come here for? We came to find and harvest pheasants. We came here to hunt birds. The idea is to put 'em up. Dogs put birds up so you have the opportunity to shoot. And that's what Web did.' "

TEMPERAMENT

"So apart from functional conformation in a Lab, we must also breed for temperament. The dog must have confidence in himself and trust his own hunches. And rapport! I have with my dogs what I call an invisible elastic band. What it amount to is it allows you to act and lets your dog react to what you do. Most dog men go about it in the opposite way. The dog acts and the handler reacts, saying 'No,' or 'Good dog,' etc. My dogs can feel the elastic band. If the dog runs too far from your control, you stop. The dog will feel it and come back in. If he's over a hill and can't see you stop, in a minute or two that band will pull tight and he'll pop back up. But if you just keep walking, he'll just keep pressing. You see this with Web all the time.

"Plus something else about temperament. You see a lot of mechanical field trial Labs . . . that's a word I got from you, Bill. The electric-shock program most field trial Labs endure (Gould and I call these trainers fry cooks) robs them of their self-confidence. It robs those dogs of their ability to work alone. They must always be under supervision.

"Now I think the American retriever field-trial people are about to pay a real heavy price for the way they've been acting. The reason is their training programs are so intense. It's pressure, pressure, pressure. And the dog has to be real tough to take it. So I see a lot of puppies coming out of these breeding programs that are frankly not suitable for everyday hunting. They are just too cranked up and they can't turn it off. But I've noticed that every really nice dog I've ever been around, and the few great ones, had an innate ability to relax.

"Take Web, for instance, you don't even know he's around. He's completely relaxed. Yet you can turn him on like a light bulb, and when he's finished what you sent him to do, he turns himself off. That's an enormous talent." And so it is.

NECK

That day on the blue grouse mountain, Web, the other Labs and Pointers, plus Mike Gould and myself, had a great hunt. Mike no longer spoke of functional conformation, but involved himself with the grouse. So let's finish out the Olympic retriever.

The angle of the neck is very important. It should hold the head high so the nose and eyes more likely avoid pollen and debris.

However, if the head is reared too far back, that tires the dog. Just as having it angle straight out front, the weight of the skull must be borne by the neck muscles.

EYES

Eyes and eyelids should be dark. It better helps the dog handle a bright sun. And it also mitigates against the cancer that you see in whiteface cattle, for example. But more important, the eyes must be balconied with a great protrusion of bone to knock away debris and keep it (if possible) from the dog's eyes.

NOSE

A dog exists for no other reason as a hunter but to carry its nose. What an uncanny instrument. For comparison, man has about 5 million smell cells. But dogs can have from 125 to 1,000 million of them. I once saw Jim Culbertson's (Jim is America's stellar amateur hunting retriever trainer and lives in Wichita, Kansas) great Lab bitch, Keg of Black Powder, wind a planted pigeon in training 200 yards to her left. Now that's a nose and that's what you want for Pup. The dog must be born with a good nose. You can enhance it in training, but you can't build it from nothing.

EARS

Too long an ear and the tip can split when the dog shakes its head: as a retriever usually does when coming from water. But too short an ear and field debris can enter the ear canal. Interesting to note, and you can check this out down the road, bird dog Hall of Famer, Jack Harper, from Benton, Mississippi, says there's a correlation between big ears and big feet, both being undesirable.

BITE

We don't want our retrievers to be either overshot or undershot. There are two reasons. The average dog with misaligned teeth has difficulty chewing hard food, but more importantly, a bitch with front teeth that don't match is too likely to pierce the belly of her pups when she's trying to gnaw loose the umbilical cord. The result is invariably death for the newborn.

TAIL SET

The higher we set the tail, the longer we extend the pelvic drive muscles that make greater runners out of our retrievers. The reach is

Web scrunches up as Gould points to high tail set, which can give you a longer pelvic drive muscle.

made by the front legs, but the drive power, the spring and the thrust, is all generated by the rear end. That's why more and more in the future we'll be seeing hunting retrievers (which must run to hunt) with what we consider to be classic Pointer tails.

TEATS AND TESTICLES

Extended teats or testicles create a hardship for a hardworking hunter. The constant abrasion against stubble, brush and coarse grass sores up the dog so that the next day it's difficult to work. You want both teats and testicles laid tight to the body.

BRAINS AND TRAINABILITY

Wehle covered intelligence for us so we'll not repeat ourselves here. But we must admit that some dogs are biddable for training and others are so hard-headed and obstinate that they tell you to forget it. And some, if you persist in trying to teach them something, will go up your arm snapping like it was an ear of corn. We decidedly don't want this dog in our training program.

HIGH PAIN THRESHOLD

We seek pups from parents that exhibit a high pain threshold. You've seen it many times: The dogs race into a cocklebur field and one turns to stone while the other, though pained, keeps on driving. This is an inheritable trait. Search for pups that have it.

SKIN

Our pup must have a loose skin that will release when snagged. A tight skin will tear. And a dermatologist will tell you the skin is the dog's house, its insulator, its protector, its bacterial barrier and its thermostat. Look for luxurious, silken coats in the parents. Skin disorders are inheritable as well as contagious.

HIPS

And finally there's hips. The nemesis of all heavy dogs, which includes our major retrievers. Buy only pups from parents that have had X-rays to determine absence of hip dysplasia. Essentially, hip dysplasia is caused by a mismatch between the hip cup and the ball of the dog's femur (thigh bone). I've had similar problems resulting in two hip replacements. The pain is tongue-biting severe. My remorse goes out to any dog with a hip problem. And so far as working—every step is sheer agony. Do all you can to make certain your pup will not develop hip dysplasia by demanding a guarantee that the parents are troublefree. The Orthopedic Foundation for Animals (OFA) is the arbiter of healthy hips in dogs inclined to hip dysplasia. The OFA screens X-rays to detect inherited hip disorders.

PROBLEMS WITH BREEDING

The sun stands high, birds fill our game bags and the self-assigned pressure to produce is lifted, so Mike Gould says, "Breeding up an ideal dog is filled with defeats. The thing I've noticed is the harder I try to improve the breeding . . . it usually gets worse [remember Wehle's drag of the race?]. The legs that seem short to me all of a sudden become way too short. Ear set was a problem, tail set was a real problem with the Labs. Length of the body compared with the length of the leg was a horrible problem. It just takes years and years to get the job done.

"For I haven't even touched the surface. There's the neck. I struggled with that for a while. I ended up with necks too long, and when I shortened them, they got too thick.

"And the chest . . ." Now Gould remembers the chest I discussed above. "We don't want a wide chest, we want a deep chest. So when the dog heats up, there's expansion for the heart and lungs. But you don't want those ribs so sprung that they're actually in a half-circle shape. You want more of a quarter-moon configuration.

"So it goes on and on. . . ."

We walk through the high alpine grass (remember, we're at 10,000 feet), the dogs make game, the blue grouse loft and we take our shots. When suddenly Gould shouts, "There's the grouse omen I've been waiting for."

"What's that?" I ask.

"The harrier. See him. He's working the grouse. But it's the strangest relationship between birds. I've never seen a harrier take a grouse, nor have I ever seen grouse shy from them. But let a redtail hawk come over and those birds go flat. Yet every time you see a harrier working in blue grouse country, get there quick . . . there are birds."

"Let's go then," I encourage. But as I look far to front, I see Web is already closing in on the harrier's sign. "No," I tell myself, "he's great . . . but that great?" To this day I still wonder.

2

Deserving the Pup You Picked

I'VE PROPOSED SPENDING more thought in picking Pup than we may do our spouses. You guys, did you measure her bite, the length of her ears, the bone balcony over her eyes? Or vice versa, what gal reading this had her husband-to-be undergo X-rays for bad hips, or checked for high toenails?

Then following all our dedication to purpose in picking Pup—we brought him home to what? If we don't have our psyche and house in order, then we'll blow the whole thing. For I can assure you this. Pups are like a bucket: You can only pour out what you've poured in. If you've not got the need or inclination to pour a lot of time and thought and effort into Pup, then let him pass. Otherwise, I can predict you'll just end up regretting the whole exercise.

SEEING THE WORLD FROM PUP'S POINT OF VIEW

Before you select a pup, you need eight things: 1) a knowledge of the critter, 2) sufficient time, 3) a place in your house Pup can call his own, 4) a private yard, 5) a car to get Pup about, 6) some old clothes, 7) a stretch of country to let Pup have Happy Time and 8) the right temperament.

SCENT MAKES SENSE

Pup knows the world through scent: His nose knows. I repeat, Pup has 125 to 1,000 million smell cells. Whereas he sees very poorly since his eye is constructed to note movement, not detail. That's why the scurrying bunny gets Pup's attention. Should the bunny sit frozen, Pup will pass it by. Unless it's upwind. Then the nose pulls the dog through the bunny's scent cone to arrive nearby, the bunny panics and leaps and now Pup can see the source of the smell and gives chase. All of which means that dogs are close-contact animals. They want to be near enough to constantly sense our odor. And that's why we call them companion animals, right? They are close-at-side to discriminate the slightest nuance in the change of our smell. And the reason for this is because pups don't discriminate all scents the same. Critical odors are those related to peril, survival of the species and food gathering.

Let's look at peril. Pups have a phenomenal discrimination of butyric acid found in human sweat. Tests show that dogs smell sweat one million times better than we do. And it's stunning to learn the average adult sweats a quart a day. Pup seeks a no-hassle life. Near-at-side he can detect our mood through our sweat. If we're placid, his sense of peril is dismissed. But should we rage, then Pup panics.

Also, dogs hear well. Humans have a hearing range up to 30,000 cycles. Dogs can perceive up to 100,000 cycles, which means they hear ultrasonic sound. This helps them locate rodents and other prey that emits high squeaks. Consider the coyote, whose primary food is the field mouse.

So there is no need to shout at a dog. He hears us better than we hear each other. My house dogs can hear footsteps in the long driveway, discriminate my wife's car engine a half-block away, detect the howls of the moving coyote pack ten minutes before they register with me and most of all, they can hear the opening of a plastic-wrapped cookie package three rooms distant.

Over the centuries the dog has become very tuned to slight nuances in human voices. This was graphically concluded by United States Army tests that discovered dogs react to a man's tired voice the same as they do to an angry tirade. This indicates to us that we should never try to train Pup when we're pooped or irritated. Our combined sweat and sound will trigger peril.

TEMPERAMENT

Throughout this book I will post laws: Tarrant's laws of dog training. These are vital laws, both true and real. *When you see a law, abide by it.* I can save you centuries of dog training errors I've learned to avoid from interviewing and going into the hunting field with experts all over the world these past thirty years. This was in addition to my own feeble efforts at trying to bring a gun dog along.

I post the first law now: *You can take the spirit out of a pup, but you can't put it back in.* And it's that spirit which will see the dog break ice for a duck, tear through bramble for a woodcock and suffer the abrasion of corn stubble all day in his persistence to put up pheasants.

Immediately that first law is followed by a second: *Nothing bad should ever happen to Pup that he can associate with a human being.* Matter of fact, this law, plus a later one involving birds, is the most important law of dog training. Which means: *Anything bad that happens to Pup because of you will rob him of his spirit.* It further means: We therefore train with our head, not our hand. We think Pup to performance, we don't try to beat him there. Okay?

The Tarrant way to train is with intimacy, not intimidation. Use reward, not punishment. We gain compliance because the dog loves us and doesn't want to break that bond. We control him by our stance, our facial expression, the tone of our voice and what we do. And always, what we do is thoughtful. We train, therefore, by personal influence.

A love-trained pup is more crushed by our turning our back on him in disappointment than all the dogs that were ever brutalized in age-old training methods. For dogs share the hurt of those they love, but a brutalized dog feels only the inadequacy and frustration of his enemy—the trainer. In love, the dog foregoes his own free will to compliance. In intimidation, the dog is forced by the punishment of the handler. Love is internal, force is external. We want duty to be felt in Pup's heart, not imprinted on his hide.

Besides, you cannot force dog or man to be a happy worker. Nor can you force self-reliance. Let a force-trained dog get out of sight of his handler, and he goes berserk trying to locate a bird. Let a love-trained dog get over a hill and he knows he has permission to self-hunt, he's been groomed to think things through himself. He, therefore, stays cool-headed and begins to exercise options and his own inherent natural genius to find the bird.

Remember Gould talked of the invisible elastic band between himself and Web? Call this ESP or whatever but realize it works. And the band can be tightened. Just let the handler step back, the band stretches and up pops the dog. Or have the handler walk in either direction sideways and the band will direct the dog the same way. The band is love and mutual respect and mutual trust: That's the way we train for the future.

The first year of Pup's life must be a honeymoon. Oh, let me step aside one moment here. You can find books that promise fast, radically new training methods. Well, this is the last thing that can be achieved—plus the most undesirable. What are you, a plumber? Did your folks give you a pipe wrench at two years of age? In other words, were you not permitted a childhood? Well, why deny Pup his? Those train-quick books have destroyed more dogs than I've been able to save. For Americans want it fast: fast food, fast banking, fast transportation. One-hour laundry! Push-button TV! Microwave dinners!

And they leap at the chance to train a dog in three months: of having a six-month-old Lab pup fetch a Canadian goose. Crap! That dog can live fifteen years. He'll make you an all-age performer. Not because you denied him his puppyhood. These are, in many ways, the best times you and Pup will have. Enjoy them.

So, I repeat, the first year of Pup's life must be a honeymoon. You are the source of his being, the dispeller of his doubts, the refuge that soothes away his fears. For look at Pup's world: He stands ten inches, you stand six feet. Lie on the floor and look up: The ceiling has now vaulted, the furniture looms overwhelmingly and a standing human is a giant. Plus the giant can reach down with one hand and swoop the pup away. In other words, Pup feels defenseless, he is totally vulnerable to anything you want to do. So he tinkles or potties on the floor and you come screaming and thud-footed, and what's left for Pup to do but cringe or bolt. To cringe is to give up spirit, to bolt is to defy you. Neither response is wanted.

So be thoughtful, gentle, patient, kind and tolerant. And being these things, you can readily see why women make the best puppy trainers. They have the softness, the lyrical voice and the passive manner to bring pups along. As do kids. Kids don't stand so tall, nor is there a threat about them in their sweat. Their shrill voices excite, their glee prompts play. Let the wife and kids have total access to Pup. They'll do more good than harm. And you'll see when you have failed, it's to one of them Pup will run. Or he'll find haven with another dog, should there be one in the house. For another ironclad law in dog training is this: *The best dog trainer is another dog.* More about this later.

TIME FOR PUP

Snatch-a-minute training is ideal for Pup until he's one year old. You're bogged down in an easy chair before the TV and Pup ambles by. Reach out and scoop him up, or let a hand dangle and stroke his head. Better yet, put your fingers in Pup's mouth. Nothing like chewing on you

Momma-dog will entrust one of these pups to you. This book will teach you what to do with it. The first requirement is your total love.

Twins Phillip and Zachary start early socializing Lab pups for their dad, professional trainer Omar Driskill.

will build intimacy in Pup's way of thinking. Chewing lets him have token dominance over you.

A commercial appears on the TV. Find the toy wedged in the crease of the chair and dangle it before Pup. Fascinate him with the dance of it and your enticing voice. Toss the toy out five feet. If Pup runs to get it, great! If not, forget it. If Pup fetches it up to run away with it, fine! If Pup brings it to you, then take it if you can. By that I mean, never pull. Always push. This gags Pup and prompts him to spit out the fetch. But to pull encourages Pup to set up and brace back and bite down. So you're doing two bad things at once: building resistance to your will and creating hardmouth.

A natural, universal trait of all dog owners is to play tug-of-war with their pups, be they Lhasa Apsos, Cairn Terriers, Cocker Spaniels, what-have-you. Well, never do it with your retriever pup. You know what I mean, don't have him set up at the end of a towel and rear back, jaws clenched, eyes glaring, as he tries to rip the towel from your hand. Or worse yet, don't entice Pup to take such a firm clench that you can swing him around in the air, Pup holding tight by his mouth. A retriever pup's mouth is the reason for his being: That's what he uses for fetch. And it must always be biddable to your wish, never sticky, never hardmouth, never resistant. So never, never, never give Pup the opportunity to learn the power of his mouth and to misuse it.

When you've finished breakfast, take five minutes in the backyard romping with Pup. Throw something for Pup if you want, or just woo him and let him chase you around the yard. Tell Pup what a great guy he is and shower with joy. For I can tell you this: Dogs learn human language. Or they learn the emotions that go with words, which communicates as well as language. I've owned dogs that have developed 300-word vocabularies through osmosis. Talk to your dog all the time: He will understand.

Also know this: Dogs love routine and dogs can tell time. Dogs want to eat, dump, play, greet you at the door and sleep in the same place at the same time every day. This is a powerful ally in dog training. Use it.

When you get home from work that night, give Pup another five minutes. And then again after supper. Maybe even before you go to bed. That would be four sessions of five minutes each—and more than enough for Pup. Any more than this will tire him. Plus, his attention span won't stretch even five minutes.

That's why quality time comes from you dropping out of the chair during a commercial and lying flat on the floor to let Pup sniff in your ear,

This ten-week-old Chesie pup can play tug-of-war with a Lab in training but not with a human involved. Benefits like this—giving Pup unlimited experiences—come from joining a hunting retrieving club.

The same Chesie pup displays the no-nonsense attitude of every good retriever, even while chewing on an old shotgun shell.

smell your breath (dogs love to smell your breath—it's a bonding ritual) and get happily roughed about by your hands. Then stand back up, take your position in the chair and either accept Pup following you or just wandering away.

In other words, you're controlling Pup's day, his world, his emotions, his movements, his activities, but not so Pup knows it or feels it or even resents it. Matter of fact, you're dog training. See how easy it is?

Another term to explain what you're doing is "imprinting." You can see this with a man who raises a clutch of ducks. The ducks believe the man is their mother and follow him everywhere.

We've now learned from working with racehorses that if you take a foal at two hours and insert your hand in his mouth thirty times, then two years later slip a bit in his mouth, the horse will accept it. Puppy breeders should be aware of this, and when each pup is born, they should insert a finger in each retriever pup's mouth thirty times to forever rid him of a reluctance to fetch. We'll later see how the breeder can further help you in training Pup by outfitting the litter with check cords at four weeks of age.

During this first year, nothing is critical in training. If Pup won't fetch, forget it. If he runs away, wave good-bye. If he shys from water, don't press it. If he leaps on you, accept it. But one thing we can't permit is for Pup to dump or tinkle in the house. So house manners are the first thing we teach.

POTTY TRAINING

Pup's a living thing fueled by food and water that must be passed out. And how you go about accomplishing house training can affect all training done in the future.

Pup must be kept in mind at all times. You must assume when he has to go and get him outside. You do this joyously, cajoling Pup, making it all fun and good times. Pick Pup up and carry him out to the same place each time and set him down. Tell Pup to tinkle or potty (yes, he will learn the words and later can even go on command). Walk Pup about. Let old smells trigger the dumping impulse. When he does go, praise him mightily. This is the most important thing to happen since the creation. Tell Pup "Good dog," leap about, encouraging him to display and jump and run and feel good about having done this thing right.

But what if it all fails? What if you're walking through the bedroom in your stocking feet and *sog,* you're in it and you leap and your impulse is to shout "Pup!" and go charging in search of him.

Don't do it. Pup got by with that one and it's your fault—not his! Got that! It's your fault. You weren't monitoring him. You weren't thinking Pup. Or you weren't reading him. Pup came to you, you saw him, but you were busy or absentminded. Then he went off and did his business. Well, he got by with this one. You do not go get him and bring him back and rub his nose in it. Never. Oh, you can bring him back and show him the spot and tell Pup ''No!'' But that's the extent of it.

That's why dog doors are an asset. And other dogs. In no time at all they'll have Pup going in and out on his own will. Or if you live in a one-pup house it's up to you to get down on your knees and coax Pup through the door flap. Leave him inside, you go outdoors, then entice him through. I've learned it's best to install two dog doors on each side of the wall. Then you have an insulating space between so cold is not readily transferred into the house.

Pup will generally tell you when he has to go. His behavior grows tense. He starts to run for no reason at all. He spins about. And then he slides his back feet up under his belly and squats. This is when you yell the most important word in dog training, ''No!'' and go quickly to scoop Pup up and get him out with all kinds of praise. That ''No!'' will be your ultimate control through Pup's life. When training with love, no harsher tactic than the spoken word will be needed. But if you have more than one dog in the house, the command ''No!'' will put them all down. So in that case you yell the offender's name, ''Pup!''

But you missed all this and the sog is in the carpet. Well, pardner, or Miss, this is our first moment of truth. If Pup's not more important than your house, you should never have brought him home in the first place. I don't mean he should have the run of the place and carte blanche destruction of whatever pleases him. What I mean is that it's no big deal. What Pup's done can be cleaned up and vanished away.

With urine, we blot it with paper towels, then (keeping a spray bottle filled with common vinegar diluted with water) we spray the spot and blot away the odor, too.

But what if it's stool or vomit? If it's runny, then mound it with table salt to suck up the moisture. Then vacuum and vinegar. Vomitted yellow bile can leave a stain, but there is a cure. Dissolve two Alka-Seltzer tablets in a half glass of warm water and scrub the stain clean.

If the stool is solid, pluck it up with toilet paper and flush it away. Once again, treat with vinegar.

After a lifetime of scooping up outdoors, I can give you some chore-proven tips. First off, you want to experiment with the several different premium dog foods to find the one you like best (knowing each time you change diets you can prompt a loose stool). Part of what you're looking for in a dog food is the production of a good, tight, small stool. That's right, some foods create more waste than others.

The second thing you need to know is how to scoop up the stool. You need a wire rake to pull the stool through grass to deposit in a dustpan contraption on a stick. Nothing works better than a common shovel on concrete. And gravel requires a solid sheet-metal scoop into the dustpan receptacle. The feces will stick to the pebbles and you'll gradually scoop to dirt.

Now what do you do with the stool you've got in hand? Well, in the city nothing works better than having a direct access to the sewer line. In the country I like to use the power takeoff on the tractor and a posthole digger, and dig several deep holes adjacent to each other. Then I throw the stool in the hole and cover with a layer of dirt. Gradually the hole fills up and you must auger new ones. There is also on the market a dog-waste disposal system. You bury a plastic "septic tank" bucket, deposit the stool, then add digesters. Waste is liquified so it goes into the earth. I've never had much luck with these tanks, but you're probably a lot brighter that I am—so give 'em a try.

So these are the things we do during the day—and in that regard, if no one's home then Pup must be left outside. No way can we ask him to wait eight, nine or ten hours.

At night we lock Pup up. A rule of dogdom is this: *Pup won't spoil his nest unless there's no alternative.* Like if he's sick. We put him in a commercial-airline-type crate in our bedroom and make him spend the night there. Next morning, first thing, we get him outdoors fast.

Should Pup cry at being locked up, then elevate the crate on a chair beside your bed and he will quiet down. You can even put a hot water bottle in there for comfort, and yes, a ticking clock does simulate the mother's heartbeat and stills some young puppies.

Incidentally, the crate has a roof on it and therefore makes a better holding area than an open cardboard box for one reason: All dogs favor something over them when resting. Note Pup—he'll more than likely sleep under the coffee table or a chair. Pups (and dogs) have a fear of attack from above. So if you're going to use a box, then partially cover it with a folded blanket. It'll settle Pup.

A FATE WORSE THAN DEATH

Repeatedly I'll explain where other trainers might be physical; you and I will work on Pup's mind, not his hide. Our instrument to assure compliance is a plain, white, plastic flyswatter. If you catch Pup in the act of tinkling on the carpet and yell "No!" then as you head toward him,

Trainer displays white plastic flyswatter to advanced dog in training. This "fate worse than death" started when Pup was just a puppy.

grab the flyswatter and tap Pup on the rump. I didn't say swat or slam or lower the boom. I said tap. That one tap can survive a lifetime (as we'll see later in this book).

I've had pups brought along this way where ten years later I could yell the dog down afield, pull the flyswatter from its recessed position down the back of my pants, raise it in display and the dog will melt to the ground in terror and submission.

For it's not the tap that does it, it's our total display of disappointment. A love-trained Pup can't accept your anger or your rejection. You're breaking his heart, not bruising his hide.

Another time the flyswatter comes in handy is when Pup barks or whines. You tell him "No noise" or "Stop that noise," order him to come to you, all the while glaring at him and displaying the swatter. I assure you Pup will grovel to you lower than a snake. It works. Use it.

PUP'S PLACE

All pups will choose their own special place in a house. Respect this decision. Let them be. At night Pup has his kennel crate, during the day he'll choose somewhere under a piece of furniture or possibly up against a wall. If he chooses a place on the carpet, then toss a folded blanket there so body oils won't discolor the fabric. And, yes, Pup needs his own toys. There should be a toy pile. Let him choose what he wants. Keep the pile stocked with cardboard rolls from toilet paper, store-bought squeakies, old slippers, even a jump rope. You never know what will turn Pup on.

But that can't be the leg of your prized dining room chair. If you catch Pup in the act, command "No!" then physically pick him up and carry him to his special place and tell him how disappointed you are in him. Should Pup persist, then rub the chair leg with a dog repellent. They're available from any pet store.

You'll find toys are not only a diversion, they are also a security blanket. Pup will feel content when a special one is near.

Now, should Pup choose your prized sofa as his special place, then tuck a beach towel into the crevices and let him have it. If Pup wants your bed, then put a baby blanket at the foot and load it with leather chew chips or toys and keep him there instead of on the bedspread.

It's up to you to pup-proof your house. If you have a spindly table with a prized vase on it, then put the thing away. You know Pup is going to knock it over. Whatever dangles, remove it, whatever protrudes, put a dog repellent on it, whatever fancy pair of party shoes is left on the closet floor, seal off by closing the closet door.

Place Pup's food bowl on an old place mat, for you know he's going to scatter kibbles. And his water dish should be placed on a towel, for Pup will drip when he drinks.

In other words, plan ahead on everything that should prompt you to eventually scream "No!" Pup'll hear enough of this in his life, so let it be reserved for something important. Let it be for bringing along a bona fide hunter, not because a pup can't resist the tassels on a doily.

Just practice common sense for the common good of the entire household. It's Pup's house, too. But let's say you can't keep Pup in the house. Well, to abandon him in the backyard will really jeopardize your training program. With the Tarrant method the good results are achieved from constant contact. Yet isolation out back may be your fact of life. So how best to house Pup? Put him in an elevated barrel. If you put every kind of doghouse ever invented in an enclosed yard and let Pup try each of them out for a week, he will eventually choose the barrel as his permanent home. Why? I don't know. That's Pup's secret. But choose the barrel he will.

Elevate yours for the following reason: With the barrel raised, Pup can crawl underneath and escape a high sun or a downpour. If it's winter and Pup wants to lounge in the faint sunlight, he can leap above the barrel to the platform. This is also the place of refuge for a dam with pups: She can escape up there and get a moment's rest.

We were once obliged to use steel or wood barrels, but now the barrel of choice is plastic or fiber glass. They're used to ship fluids, powders, etc. Buy one from your local junkyard and *make sure it held no toxic chemicals*. Whatever barrel you buy that had benign contents, take the barrel to the car wash and blast it out good. Cut out half the lid (if there is one) so when the barrel is laid horizontally the bottom of the entry is a half-door. This lip will keep straw, cedar chips or other bedding from scattering about the yard.

But remember, out of sight is usually out of mind. Now it's your obligation to spend even more time with an outdoor Pup so he becomes an extension of your being.

A PRIVATE YARD

Pup's natural environment is the out-of-doors. Pup must have a piece of land he can call his own. Some place he can dig in the flower garden, and fetch up pebbles to bring into the house, and find favorite places to dump. It's also your kindergarten playground where Pup re-

K-9 Kastle updates the old barrel with half-lid entry for Pup. This model shows barrel, flapping entrance (which can be locked) and sunroof—all that's wrong with this model is there's no room beneath for Pup to find shelter from sun and rain.

ceives first instructions on good manners. Here he'll learn to heel, sit, stay, come and even fetch.

But in the beginning Pup won't learn these things formally. Rather, they will come about through osmosis, which Webster tells us is "the tendency of a solvent to pass through a membrane," or in human terms, "an apparently effortless absorption of ideas, feelings, attitudes, etc., as if by biological osmosis."

In other words, do we as humans learn to drive a car that day we sit beside a driving instructor, or have we through a childhood of watching mom and dad already gotten a pretty good idea of what to do? The answer is obvious. Much of what we know has come through osmosis. And that's what we want for Pup.

And again you can see the benefit of having other dogs about. Pup can see them heel, sit, stay, come and fetch. And he'll want in on the action. For he sees what they do pleases you and he can't stand being ignored. That's why another law is: *A dog trainer can train thirty dogs easier than he can train one.*

But we've all started with one pup and did the best we could. That's probably where you are and it's *you* I want to help. Repeatedly we'll show how the pros benefit from a kennel of dogs, but we'll not forsake you with only one. We'll get your pup trained. That's a promise.

Another benefit of a yard that Pup can call his own is *nature.* Pup can learn he has a nose, learn which way the wind blows, scent the good earth, puzzle over the passing toad, learn that roses prick, chase a butterfly, see a bird and wonder at the strange fascination that rises in his breast. And most of all, he can have good times with you. Happy Times. For here you run and leap and lie down and roll over and yell and become the most important and the most intriguing thing in Pup's life. Again he learns you're no threat. And you exist only for his pleasure. Unless he displeases you. Then he sees the hurt eyes, the gulp, the bitten lower lip, and he comes submissively to you, trying to make things right, for he can't accept breaking your heart.

A PLACE IN THE COUNTRY

Pup must learn the territory. Pup must have a place in the country where he can run to the skyline and stumble through ditches and snag on barbed wire and shy from the milk cow and stick his nose in the sheet water to fetch a shining stone. For here is where Pup learns he has legs and lungs and heart and nose. Here he learns the sheer exultation of running with the wind and leaping clumps of grass and flushing up the meadowlark.

Two Lab pups learning the territory.

I call this Happy Timing. And through Pup's life he must have this-.And so must you. It does you both good to walk on the soft earth and smell the country air all rich with cow dung and wet grasses and blooming brush.

Here Pup will learn he has a right- or left-hand lead. He'll learn that when he jumps a ditch, his left leg always comes down first. So if he wants to run in a straight line he'll compensate since that left leg will usually give and veer him to the left. Later on this asset will keep him on line when you send him for a bird he didn't see fall.

In other words, everything we do is training Pup for the future—but Pup doesn't know it. So we get grudgeless performance. And we're not the heavy. It's all done with Happy Times.

Pup's learning something else that will be vital to his hunting life. Know what it is? Guess. That's right, he's learning he can't catch a flyaway bird. How valuable this will be when you shoot a Canadian goose that goes into a one-mile death glide and Pup wants to give chase. Only there's a major highway en route. We can't have Pup hit by a car.

Happy Timing lets Pup's world disappear. This is important. In later life he'll have encountered everything unique in the wild and not be distracted while hunting or on retrieve. It's like me. I have a writing room. I don't move a thing in that room. For my eye will go to whatever's new or different and break my concentration. The bird has to be Pup's sole mission. He can't be stopping to piddle around sniffing something en route. Pup will have sniffed it all by the time he's a year old.

MUD

You can know a hunter by how well he wears his mud. Same goes for a hunting retriever. Which means your clothes and your car must also be Pup-proof.

Pup needs a crate in your wagon. An enclosed crate. For he will get in there and shake and splatter your interior. Avoid the wire crates, get a plastic one and even tape the air holes shut. Pup can still breathe through the wire door. There's just no sense in messing up the family car with a mud-shaking dog.

Protect the carpeting by installing a rubber runner bought from any janitorial supply company. You can even leave it extralong at the back door. Then you can flip it out to hang down over the bumper and give Pup greater purchase while he's leaping to kennel.

But heed this warning: Pup can take a ton of cold compared to an ounce of heat. The interior of a closed car in a high sun can reach 150

Author's pack is released for Happy Timing. Puppies will go along when they can keep up.

Until then, pups will have their own special outings.

Heard of guys or gals who have gone to the dogs? Well here's a car that did.

degrees. So never go off and leave Pup locked up in a sealed car. It is a customary practice of professional trainers with dogs housed in compartments behind the truck cab to put a block of ice in each unit. If you're transporting Pup over long distances in a car that has no air conditioning you should do the same. Once again, you have to think more of Pup than you do your possessions. Sure the ice will melt and water will run out, so you'll just have to sop it up and wring it out.

Since Pup will spend a great part of his time wet—and shaking—I find it more comfortable to wear plastic or rubber chaps when working him. You can buy them at any gun dog supply store. They're either tube-legged that you pull on and cinch to your belt, or they zip up the side and you don the opened material then close it up. If I'm out walking with wet legs in a cold wind, I tense up. Also, I shy away from a wet retriever when he's sitting to side and handing me the duck. I know the dog is going to stand and shake just as soon as I take the bird from him. But we can't be tense, nor shy away, when Pup's trying to please us. Pup will sense it. So dress for the wetness and stay relaxed and receptive to Pup's shaking.

Well, that's it. We've looked at the eight imperatives necessary in Pup's life. And we've got him settled into the house, playing in the backyard and going for long, productive walks in a field. Now we get to yard training. Learning what to do begins on the next page.

Heidi Pittman, assistant to Omar Driskill, displays an age-old yard training method. She first commands the dog to heel and walk along side.

3

Yard Training

$\mathbf{M}$Y WIFE, DEE, is a doll. As a gun dog trainer who tries to write, I must be very cautious in my feeble use of words. But Dee is my eternal joy by her constantly mangling figures of speech. When I'm in a book, I'm lost to her for months. So the other morning she asked me, "Where are you? Second field?"

"Second field?" I replied, laughing. "Where's that?"

"That's beyond last field," she quipped, unfazed by my making fun of her.

You and I and Pup have done so well up till now I sure don't want the two of you ending up in second field. So let's get yard training straight.

THE PUP YOU RAISED

I'm going to show you how the pro does it and how you should do it. You see, you have the benefit of bringing Pup along from a baby, but not the poor pro. He sees the neglected dog at one year of age and the owner tells him, "I want my dog doing it all in one month." So the pro who accepts such an impossible assignment usually trains with force, not tact. He must compel the dog to performance, not love the dog to it. But then, you, yourself, may have come by an older dog that will require

Now Heidi stops, saying heel again. Dog sits.

If not, she presses his rump down with her nongun hand.

Then she tosses out check cord...

...and tells dog to stay by voice and hand displayed before his face.

Now she goes to the far end of the check cord —still displaying traffic cop hand signal—and picks up cord...

...which she now milks in immediately after telling the dog to come. Her next sequence will be to tell the dog heel and start all over.

some manhandling. So we'll look at every possible way of getting the job done. Okay?

HEEL

The first command taught is heel. That means for Pup to sit beside your nongun side (if you're a left-handed gunner, he goes to the right, and vice versa). The reason for this is evident. Whatever your major side is, that's where you'll hold the gun when Pup retrieves. Your free hand will be on the nongun side.

And how does Pup sit? Squared away, facing front, with no angle to his body. Plus, the base of his neck will be immediately adjacent to the stitched seam in your pants leg. That gets his head out far enough so he can see across your body, but not far enough to entice him to break.

Now outfit Pup with a strong, heavy-duty leather or nylon collar with a welded D-ring to accept the cord or leash. Don't use a chain-choke collar. Nothing could be more injurious for a retriever. When contracted it compresses the throat and larynx and can severely injure the dog. For we're going to be handling a great deal of force through this collar. Pup is going to leap and strain, and we want a flat belt of leather or nylon to dispense the pressure. And don't worry if the leather collar gets wet. Your boots are made of leather and they're wet, aren't they?

Also, there's another collar that can be used. Ignored by most trainers and even outlawed in Great Britain, the pinch collar can be used in severe cases such as with an older, recalcitrant dog entering training. We're talking of the spike collar with all the spikes filed pointless. Then when Pup strains, the collar closes because of pressure against the connected leash, and this angles the blunt points to pinch the skin. But let Pup quit his struggle and the collar pops open, the pinch gone.

I mention this collar since some pros with sensitive hands can use it and you may see pictures of it in this book. But I don't want you to use it. Too many first-time dog trainers don't have the timing or finesse to use it properly. *And I don't want Pup hurt.* After you've trained several dogs, you might find a use for the pinch collar and incorporate it in your program, but not now. We're going to do the whole thing with the wide, flat leather or nylon collar.

THE CHECK CORD

Now you need to make a check cord. Twenty-two feet rolls right on the arm, and with this you'll teach Pup to quarter afield. But right now we

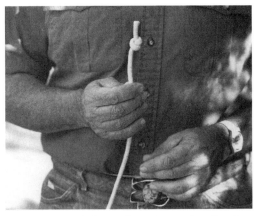

This sequence of photos shows how to tie a litter-box check cord. Tie an overhand knot in the end of the cord.

Now a few inches down tie an open overhand knot...

...through which you slip the knotted end.

Now cinch up so loop fits Pup's neck.

need a check cord of no more than six feet. Buy some strong ½-inch nylon cord with plenty of body. If the cord is limp, then throw it in a mud puddle overnight and let it dry with authority. At the end of the cord tie a brass snap swivel (bought at any gun dog supply or nautical supply store). At the other end tie an overhand knot so that when Pup bolts and the cord slides through your hands there'll be a stop.

Now snap the short cord to Pup's collar and coax him about the yard. Go with him. If Pup pulls you, race to catch up; if Pup bulls up and sits, then you stand and wait. This will be his show, so let Pup have a free hand. Do this over and over: Remember snatch-a-minute training. *Now all dog training is point of contact, repetition and association.* Our point of contact is Pup's neck. Our snatch-a-minute training is repetition. And our association is our voice giving the appropriate command. Until one day Pup will run without the cord and respond to our voice.

That's why the litter box check cord is so valuable. Let's explain it. At four, five or six weeks of age each pup in the litter is outfitted with a two-foot-long check cord. These are made from ⅜-inch nylon cord. Tie an overhand knot in one end, loop the cord about the pup's neck, poke the knot through a cinching honda in the trailing cord. Tied this way the knot can't slip and choke Pup. The trailing cord becomes his first leash—his calamity at first, your salvation later.

For watch what happens. A puppy moves, he inches about. Another pup sees the white check cord slide by. He slaps it with a paw. Now he puts it in his toothless jaws and is pulling. The leashed pup is stopped in his tracks and can't believe it. He pulls and can't go anywhere. Now he comes undone, screaming in puppy voice, "Mommy, mommy . . . the world has come to an end . . . save me . . . save me . . ."

Then the leashed pup jerks loose or the anchor pup lets go, and the victim tumbles head over tail. Then for a second he broods about it. For nothing in life likes to lose freedom. That's what education is all about. Removing self-will. Gaining compliance that is pleasant and useful to group life. But it's no fun and we all hate it. And so does Pup. He wants to be free.

Now the victim sees a littermate's cord go by, grabs, it and starts the other way. The lassoed pup sets up, front paws braced, neck bowed, butt tucked under, eyes bulged out. And he's dragged across the litter box.

What's important here is that all pups are learning to give to the lead. How much better that Pup's own kind be the culprit that teaches him, rather than you. For remember, *nothing bad can ever happen to Pup that he can associate with a human being.* This is our first instance of

Advanced puppies frolic around feed bowl wearing their litter-box check cords. By now they've all learned to give to the lead and bear no grudge against any human.

situating Pup among others of his own kind so they can be assistant trainers. It's magnificent dog training. Nothing can equal it.

A week or two of litter-box check cording and you can walk in, pick up a trailing leash and heel a pup away. No grudge, no balk, no problem. I've even done it with coyote pups. That should be proof enough of how well the system works.

Then you buy one of these litter box check-corded pups and he's already learned to give to the lead. How much better that will make our yard training. All Pup's fight was vented on his own kind. He just naturally complies for you.

Okay, let's teach heel. There will come a day when Pup's giving well to the lead and not flying hither and yon and there is some degree of compliance about him. Grasp the short check cord down near the collar and, saying "Heel," carousel Pup about you until he's standing adjacent to the seam of your nongun pant leg.

But just a minute. What's this carousel? That's letting Pup walk across the front of you, to your gun side, then behind you to arrive at your nongun side, where you want him. Sometimes pups will naturally do this one or more times. Sometimes you will intentionally carousel Pup about you to settle him down and to get him situated exactly like you want him at heel.

Now Pup's at heel, and should he bolt, then pull him back. If Pup darts to side, reel him in. If Pup rears back, pull him forward. If Pup crowds your knee, then push him out. Then shake it all off and let Pup have free rein to walk about the yard. Now repeat the drill. Over and over. Drill, rest, drill, rest. Then put it away until the next day.

Finally, when Pup's heeling, tell him to sit. To gain compliance, pull up on the cord with you gun hand and, stooping over, press Pup's rump down with your free hand—the thumb and fingers making a bridge that spans the vertebrae just before the hips. Pull the cord, thrust down on the hips and Pup'll sit. Repeat over and over.

But know this. You can ruin a pup with too much yard training. He'll be so nonfield-oriented, and wanting to please you so much, he'll want to play this game instead of seeking birds. So all yard training must be mixed well with long stretches of Happy Timing afield. There is no other way.

TRAINING WHISTLE

Until now we've handled Pup with oral commands. But over long distances in a high wind, amidst heavy cover, or while Pup's immersed in wave-tossed water, the whistle carries better than the human voice. It can even evidence emotion when your cheeks are ballooned, your eyes bulged and your forehead purple.

Choose a whistle akin to the big (not the small) English-made Acme Thunderer. This is a pea whistle with terrific carrying capability. It costs a pittance. Hang one or two on the lanyard of your choice and now you look like a dog trainer.

Whistle commands are one long blast for sit and a series of one medium-long blast and toots for come in. For instance, sit is *tweeeeeet.* And come in is *tweet-toot-toot-toot.* Or said another way, sit is *daaaaaaah,* where come in is *dah, dit, dit, dit.* Okay?

Now you have Pup at heel, and instead of telling him to sit, you blow the whistle. You needn't use so much volume when Pup's close at side: Save the blast for distant needs. Your ultimate control will come when Pup's hunting distant and you whistle for him to sit, then give him (what retriever trainers call the suck-in whistle) the come-in whistle. This is done by your constantly repeating the whistle command while you're bent over and coaxing Pup with a begging arm; that is, the arm and hand are raised before you as high as your breast, then dropped down to your side, this being done over and over. The action of the arm is akin to milking in a rope, where you reach and grasp then pull to your side, then reach and grasp and pull to your side.

But the test of it all is for Pup to come when the come is in you and not in Pup: You want him to come, but he has other ideas.

COME

First off, while living your lives together inside the house, you've given Pup oral commands for whatever he's doing. If it's coming toward you, you've said come. If he's starting to sit, then you've said sit. The commands were issued when the behavior was exhibited by the dog.

All this is transferred outdoors. When Pup turns from the far side of the yard and heads toward you, tell him come.

But there'll come a day when Pup's going the other way and you say come—and he'll keep on going. And this can't be, for it's raining and you're getting soaked and Pup won't potty and now he's going to roll in the mud.

On a dry day there'd be two things you could do. You could kneel down. Remember, Pup's had the joy of investigating you as you've lain on the floor. That was fun. Seeing you lower yourself, he'll come running. Or you can even lie down. But let's say all this doesn't entice Pup to come. Okay, turn your back on Pup and appear to run away by running in place. Remember, Pup's eyes register movement better than detail. He'll believe you're leaving him and come running. You're glancing back and down, and when you see him pass, reach down and scoop him up.

USE OF THE CHECK CORD

But finally you'll outfit Pup with the twenty-two-foot check cord snapped to the D-ring of his flat collar. When Pup's sitting, you'll throw the long cord out to front, then telling Pup to stay, you'll walk to front, carrying the cord in your hand (letting it slip through as you walk), turn about, pull the cord and say either "Come" or "Heel." Some trainers even prefer the command "Here." Choose what you want. But more than likely Pup will want to come with you and will not stay seated. We'll teach stay later but right now this is the gentlest way to teach come, for you're not working a moving dog. A moving dog has go-away force, counterforce, and something's got to give when you say come. You either let the rope be jerked from your hand or Pup can be flipped down and freak out. We want neither.

So Pup's distant and moving, and you blow the come-in whistle or vocally command come and give a slight tug on the check cord. This will turn Pup's head toward you, then you either kneel or lie down or run in place to entice Pup near your side.

But never jerk the cord so as to abruptly wheel Pup about or knock him off his legs. This isn't our style. How can you expect him to come if you've hurt him distant from you? He'll want to run further away, not come back.

Finally the day will come when you can face Pup, standing up, give the come command and then milk him in. By that I mean always extend your nongun hand to hold the check cord, then milk it through quickly with your gun hand. This is much faster than trying to milk with both hands. Pup can't run faster than you can gather in the cord, which means he's not going to tangle or drag the cord. He'll be running free.

The next step will be to order come with Pup running free of the check cord. There are two things you can do—it depends on Pup. One, you can blow the sit whistle, get compliance, then entice Pup near to side. Or, two, you can blow the whistle, get Pup to look at you, then pretend to run away so he'll follow.

But you never, never, never chase Pup. This compounds the problem. Being chased is a game Pup will want to play. Never let Pup experience it. Always go the other way when Pup refuses to come. Or hide. That's right, duck behind a bush or around the corner of the house. Call Pup—his curiosity will bring him to you.

I don't care how intimate your relationship has been with Pup, there will come a day he'll try you. There's always an attempt by Pup to see just who's in charge: you or him. You've called Pup to come, he's ignored you, and kneeling or lying down or hiding accomplishes nothing, so now you must be the heavy.

The greatest puppy trainer that ever lived is momma-dog. She controls her brood through mock malice, lips thinned, the white of her canines gleaming, her eyes but slits, her hackles raised as she stands directly above the errant pooch and growls down on him with the hot breath of opprobrium (which Webster defines as ". . . anything bringing disgrace"). That is, momma-dog is shaming Pup to good behavior. And we do, too. Ours is all bark and no bite. But Pup will react to our displeasure and our display as surely as he reacts to the show put on by his mother.

THE DAY OF RECKONING

So this is the moment of truth, and we yell in a voice that could move earth and ocean, "Pup . . . No!" This will usually drive Pup to ground, and you start running. And you're coming heavy-footed, yelling every step of the way and flailing your arms, and when you get to Pup you give him sheer hell. "What's the matter with you? You an idiot or something? You can't hear me? Is that it? Well, you better hear me, you hear that? I mean it. I'm not going to put up with this crap." And it goes on and on with Pup groveling on the ground, finally turning over to expose his belly in total submission. Then you tell him to heel and sit and stay (more on stay later), then you walk back to where you first called him in and yell, "Pup . . . Come." He should approach like a jet.

Let me emphasize, however, all our word commands are not spoken as by a cartoon Indian: "Come," "Ugh," "Stay," etc. What do we want to convey? Maybe a terse one-word order is vital. But much more likely, especially when Pup is older, are enticing, playful, congenial sentences. "Hey, Pup, come over here." "Now I've told you and told you . . . I want you to heel." Yes, dogs will pick out key words. *Sentences do not confuse, they enhance.* "You better come here" carries a lot of import.

As does, "Now, Pup, you know better than that. I told you heel, now heel."

I've said before that there's seemingly no limit to the words a close-contact dog can learn. My buddy Bill Berlat, his tip-a-Sherman-tank Chesie named Gunner and I have just spent the last five days hunting turkey. No, Gunner was not in the field. He rode in the Suburban, standing on the back platform, with his head above the front seat. Bill would say to Gunner, "Give me a hug," and the behemoth would lay his barrel head on Bill's shoulder. This is the result of constantly having your dog with you: Take him to the grocery or on a trip to town, let him run alongside the car on a pasture lane. There's just no other thing so important as having your dog with you as much as you can.

SHAMING AS PUNISHMENT

But consider what we've done. We've disgraced Pup, we haven't beaten him. Matter of fact, we didn't even touch him. It was all done by our approach, our physical stance, the butyric acid in our sweat, our facial expression and the doom in our voice. And that's dog training.

Thus you can see why Pup must be raised in the house. He must be so bonded to you he can't stand your displeasure.

If he's made you mad, if he's disappointed you, he must feel the shame of this. For he can't stand your wrath, he can't stand your displeasure or your rejection or your scolding. His heart is broken, his hide is not beaten. And that broken heart hurts more than all the lickings ever given. The light of his life has spurned him. A calamity akin to the sun not coming up one morning for us. Pup's love and dependency is too strong to allow alienation.

Did it ever amaze you that dogs know where your eyes are? It has me. And they know what the eyes mean. It's uncanny. They're more attuned to eyes than humans. I can show but a hint of displeasure in my eyes and put my entire string down. With no more display than that. Start to notice. All the time you're with Pup he'll be checking your eyes. And it's been noted in African journals that strong eye contact can even turn a lion. Show them you're fearless and they'll sometimes turn away and leave you alone. Show Pup you're mighty damned upset and he disassembles. Oh, he'll come crawling and gulping and begging. And accept a little of his contrition but don't overplay your hand.

Release Pup with a clap of the hands, saying something like "All right." Let Pup know all's forgiven but not to let it happen again.

It's imperative you know how to read Pup, you know what his body language is saying. When Pup is placed in positions of stress, he will gulp and lick his top lip with his tongue. When he finally gives in, he'll sigh. Same as us. When we've finally accepted our fate, we, too, sigh. We throw up our hands, take a deep breath and let all the wind out. But not Pup. He shows defeat by relaxing his shoulder muscles. Watch him closely. Pup is yours when the gulping and licking stop and the shoulders sag. You just won.

Then you must immediately bring Pup back up. He's already given up, no need to rub it in.

THE POWER BAR

Mike Gould, the pro we hunted blue grouse with in Chapter 1 gives us a simple, effective device to achieve heel, sit, stay, but there is this caution: The device generates great power and must be used with a mellow mind and a sensitive touch. I reveal its existence and application not because you'll ever need it if all goes well with Pup, but what if there's a hitch? What if something just isn't right and Pup continues to defy you? Or maybe you've taken in an older dog that needs more force in training?

This is how you make a power bar and put it to work. The power bar is a lever used to overcome resistance at one end by holding fast the other end and applying pressure at some point along the lever: that spot being the fulcrum. An example would be the common household broom. You hold the top end in your right hand (should you be right-handed), and the stationary point (or the fulcrum) is your clutched left hand, while the resistance is the bent-back bristles brushing the floor.

To make a power bar, cut and fit a piece of ½-inch electrical conduit as follows: Place one end of the conduit in your gun hand and lodge that hand in your solar plexus. Let the conduit hang straight down. Cut it off six inches below the crotch of your pants. I am five feet, eight inches tall and my power bar is twenty-four inches long. That'll give you an idea of relative length.

Through the open tube of the conduit, slide a ⅜-inch nylon cord. At the bottom end wrap it around a brass swivel snap and feed the cord back through the tube. It extends out the top end of the conduit where you tie the looped-back cord in a granny knot to the main check cord. The check cord should extend from the power bar about twenty feet, tossed over your shoulder, and left to drag behind you on the ground.

Mike Gould's power bar system of yard training illustrated on this and the next three pages, begins with a bar looped to a swivel snap and tied off at the other end of the bar.

The bar is settled in trainer's solar plexus while his nongun hand bumps and taps the bar to get Pup to heel.

When trainer stops and says heel, the dog must sit.

If he doesn't, then the power bar is lifted above dog's neck and angled down in front...

...This forces dog to sit. When dog is walked in a circle to the left, however, the bar must be placed across the trainer's lap to keep the dog from veering out.

Dog is told to stay and handler moves to front. If dog moves, handler anchors him by stepping on angled bar. Then handler backs off, still saying stay...

...then he commands come and flips the bar up and...

...milks the cord in as Pup rushes forward.

TEACHING HEEL

Okay, position Pup beside you, clasp the top of the power bar to your chest with your gun hand and place your other hand either on the snap swivel or just above it on the bar. Command heel and step off, ever ready to bump the power bar with your nongun hand and startle Pup to compliance. The bump is made by the V of your extended thumb and forefinger.

Should Pup jump to side, tap him back in. If he rears back, tap him forward. If he leaps in front, tap him rearward. If he crowds your leg, bump him out. The bar generates great power, so our taps are minimal. And never is our pressure maintained. Tap and release, tap and release.

Walk Pup in a great circle to the right (assuming you're right-handed). This will keep him naturally distant, whereas if you walk him in a left-hand circle, Pup would be inclined to crowd your knee since you'd be moving into him. Just tap the bar when Pup hesitates and keep him moving. As always, our training sessions are short with sweetening-up time interspersed.

To walk Pup in a left-hand circle for a right-handed gunner, the bar must now be carried parallel to the ground while your lap forms the fulcrum. This keeps Pup extended so you're not walking into his side. Again the nongun hand is used to tap in, back, out and forward.

After adequate sessions of teaching heel, we now ask Pup to sit. We stop, he does, too, then we command sit, and lowering what has been the top end of the bar toward the ground and elevating the nongun hand high above Pup's head, we push the lever back. Pup must automatically sit.

STAY

Now it's one thing to ask Pup to sit but something even more stressful to command he stay seated. Once again we're taking freedom from Pup, and we recall the six-week-old puppy the first time he was stopped by the trailing litter-box check cord. Who among us hasn't had a grade-school teacher tell us to sit down and be quiet! We complied with a pouty grudge.

In our first method of teaching heel, sit, stay with nothing but a limp cord, we tell the seated Pup to stay and then step around before him, hand raised, voice commanding in a steady tone, over and over, stay, stay, stay. Our stance and demeanor is that of a traffic cop: He's in the inter-section with the whistle in his mouth, hand raised, his face showing he means business.

Gradually we work further and further away. But what happens when we're ten feet distant and Pup steps forward? We command him to sit, he refuses to comply, so we go to Pup, physically pick him up and replace him in the exact spot he vacated. Don't think Pup doesn't have an uncanny sense of place. He does. For example, it's almost impossible to return a dog to any locale he's been hurt. He associates the place with the pain. I once had a retriever named Happy get hung up on a trot line. That's a catfish rigging where a long line is extended between two fixed points and along its length hangs a series of short lines with baited hooks.

Happy was swimming and his downward thrust compelled a hook completely through his forearm. I cut him loose and carried him to the house, where I removed the hook while Happy sat on the picnic table. But the point I want to make is this: At no time ever again would Happy enter water at the site of the trot line.

So we've returned Pup to his sitting spot and backed away, and like a traffic cop, told him to stay, but, oops, here he comes again. Well, this can't be, so now we outfit our check cord with a bowline knot. The knot is tied that length from the swivel snap so its bulk is immediately below the end of Pup's jaw. Now we step off and watch Pup's shoulder muscles, for they must move before he can lift a paw. We see a twitch and throw a wave down the check cord to arrive with an upper thud of the bowline knot against Pup's chin. The tap startles him, breaks his concentration, he forgets what he was going to do and, eureka, he sits!

But long before introducing the bowline knot to Pup, we've practiced throwing the wave by snapping the check cord to a garage door, the bumper of our car, the wrought-iron posts in a gate. It takes split-second timing to be a dog trainer. That's why you must be able to read the dog. The shoulder muscles twitch, and you snap the wave down the cord. If you're late, then Pup's already stood. You want to get him coming up. And you want the bowline knot to snap up with authority. You don't want it to swing out and miss Pup's jaw.

Eventually you'll tell Pup to stay, drop the check cord and go around the corner of the house. Be considerate, don't go there and read a book. Just stay a minute and reappear. Then return to Pup and praise him, really lay it on, for quite frankly he's just given you another bit of his freedom and that's a hard thing to do.

TEACHING STAY WITH THE POWER BAR

With the power bar, stay is simplified. You merely tell Pup to stay, step around in front, bringing a dangling bar along with you, then drop your end to the ground, which forms a wedge against Pup's collar, and back off (once again like the traffic cop with hand raised), continually saying "stay."

In this instance Pup can't follow. He can't even rise. If he starts to move forward, the wedged power bar forces him back down.

But let's say Pup tests you. Instead of coming straight forward, he turns to side to rise. Never mind, just flip the bar up with the check cord and toss it over to wedge Pup at his new angle. Once again, Pup can't move.

You reinforce all this by coming up close to Pup, and each time you say stay, press down on the angled and wedged bar with your nongun foot. Press, say stay. Press, stay. Over and over.

Then when you're ready for Pup to come, order just that, flip the end of the bar out of its bite in the earth and milk Pup to you.

CHECK CORDING

The power bar is also an asset in teaching Pup to quarter before you, to blanket a field in search of bird scent. First you unclip the power bar from Pup's flat collar, then put a snap on the opposite end of the check cord (yes, you'll need to provide a second snap). Now there's some twenty feet between the power bar and Pup. Then you cast Pup right, and when he reaches the end of the check cord, you command "Ho," or "Hup"; then when Pup glances back to see what you want, you step off in the direction for him to go and give the power bar a pull in that direction.

"Ho" is a bird dog handler's term used to turn a dog afield. "Hup" is a spaniel trainer's term used to tell the dog to stop, sit, stay, but bird dog trainers use it to tell the dog to look up or attend or to know something afield is about to happen, that is, to look sharp. Use whichever fits your tongue and your psyche best. I prefer "Ho" since it can be said with a grunt near the dog but sung as a *HOOO-ooo* when Pup's far distant afield. Bird dog handlers use it both ways: "Ho" to turn a close dog and *HOOO-ooo* (which is a long plaintive singsong) to let the far-reaching bird dog know where the handler is so the dog can check back in from time to time.

Once again the bar will generate great pressure. Here's how you hold the bar: Center the top end in your solar plexus with your gun hand as you have before. But now the bar is extended straight out to your left side. You tell Pup to cast right, the oral command for this is "Back," or if you're going to be working more than one dog at a time, then cast by using Pup's name. Pup casts right and is nearing the end of his check cord when you yell "Ho," and as Pup turns, you pivot and step off left while at the same time pulling the far end of the extended bar with your left hand.

As Pup courses before you, the bar is shifted so the nongun hand holds one end at the solar plexus and the other end extends right. Again Pup nears the end of his cord, so you yell "Ho," and when he turns to see what you want, you pivot and step off right, giving the bar a tug to force Pup in that direction.

Together you lace the field.

Later this training technique has great transfer, for you whistle Pup to stop, but just before he sits, you yell "Ho" and step off in the direction you want him to go, and you've got the arm up that held the extended power bar to further indicate what you want Pup to do.

Well, we've learned a lot, you and me, but Pup has yet to get it all down. So respect this. Be patient with Pup, let him have lots of Happy Timing to shake it all off and always before ending any training session, sweeten Pup up with frolic.

We're a quarter of the way through this book now and so far we've worked Pup as an obedience dog. There has been no emphasis on hunting. But from now on, duplicating a day's hunt afield will be the sole and express purpose of everything we teach. For example, I'll mention two things. So far we've stood beside Pup in all our teaching of heel, sit, stay and come. But when hunting dove and duck afield, we sit. So that's how we'll train–sitting. Which has the advantage of lowering us to Pup's level. Also, we've used the human voice for every command. No more. Instead of sending a bird boy to hurrah and get Pup's attention the way we used to do, now we'll have him blow a duck call before throwing either a duck or a pigeon. Pup's a bird dog . . . we'll use a bird call to attract him.

It all boils down to this. If you want to hunt like you trained, then you must train like you hunt. Omar Driskill, founder of the hunting retriever movement in America, professional hunting retriever trainer, duck camp operator and guide, says, "Training is like boot camp for a dog, but opening day of the bird season is Vietnam. It's the real thing. Your ability as a trainer is for Pup to not note any difference. His first duck blind in actual hunting should be his one-thousandth duck blind in training. If you've trained the dog right, there'll be no surprises for him should you be going for pheasant, grouse, woodcock, ducks, geese or bobwhite."

4

Fetching the Dummy

PUP KNOWS THE RUDIMENTS of heel, sit, stay, come, no and no noise, as well as his name. Something else you've been working on I've not mentioned is "Kennel." Every time you want Pup to enter a door, a car, a kennel crate, a boat or what-have-you, the order is "Kennel," which is taught by opening the door, pointing into the opening and giving the oral command. In the beginning you'll physically have to put Pup where you want him, but "Kennel" is an order quickly learned.

Pup may not know each command all that well: He just has passing glimpses of what they all mean. And Pup is probably six months to a year old. I admit there are precocious pups that knock this timetable askew, as there are dullards.

I remember River Oaks Corky (his picture hangs on my wall), the immortal black Lab who achieved over 500 field trial points. Folks, that's a ton. When Corky was a pup, his trainer, a Chicago printer named John Trzepacs, would hide duck and pheasant wings in his home basement and order Corky down to find them. But Corky was too bright. He'd listen upstairs to John's footsteps and know right where to go. Or he'd cheat and peek down the stairs. So John would hide the wings four feet high and Corky would have to search for them standing on his hind legs.

And in the parlor Corky was taught to fetch dimes. John explains, "Sometimes I'd have to tell him more than once before he'd spit up the dime and hold it in his teeth for me to retrieve.'' Well, we can't all be perfect.

When Corky was but five months old, John had him jumping off four-foot-high sea walls into storm-tossed Lake Michigan. And they'd walk the beaches together each morning, the man firing a blank pistol, Corky retrieving dead birds that dogless hunters had killed and never brought to hand the day before.

So this book is not written for the Corkys of the world, or for the pup that Bob Wehle mentioned up front ''that couldn't manage the kennel gate.'' I write for the average pup. But I ask you to realize that an all-age dog usually doesn't come into his own as a hunting journeyman until he's three to four years old. You've got time.

I remember Judy, a black bitch of mine who couldn't find her feed pan in a fifty-mile gale. I recall the day I sent her for a mark (a thrown bird she was supposed to *mark* down), and she leveled the grass—just tramped it flat—trying to find the bird. Whereas a two-year-old Peekapoo named Muffy was standing in the kennel truck cab with her front paws on the dash—and she was whining. I finally let her out, and she raced across the field to fetch up the bird and drag it back to the casting line. Judy was given to a farmer down the road. I took Muffy quail hunting.

THE MARK

Pup's a finished hunting retriever coursing milo stubble when he flushes a cock pheasant, neon feathers glittering in the prairie sun—you can hear the thuds of his wing beats as he strives to climb and catch a sailing wind—the cackle of his alarm warns others of his kind of their own impending fate, and the shotgun booms. Down the pheasant comes in a plop and burst of dust, and Pup is off in hot pursuit. He has *marked* the bird. He saw it fall, registered in his mind the exact spot and took off in hasty pursuit.

Or Pup's sitting to side in a duck blind, a red-legged mallard drake (redlegs are always the last to blow down from their northern haunts) buzzes your blind and you're hunkered down, just part of one of your eyes is showing, and Pup's sitting tall, whimpering, shivering in anticipation as you raise and fire, and the drake folds in midair, plummets and scuds across the pond's surface. ''Back,'' you yell, and Pup launches to fetch the duck he's *marked* down.

Back? you query.

Yes, ''Back.'' That means for Pup to get back. It was given to us by the Briton who had stopped his retriever afield, raised his hand as a visual signal and commanded "Back," which meant for Pup to get further back—the dog was hunting short of the mark.

THE FIRST RETRIEVE

I've grudgingly let you toss things for Pup in the house and the backyard, but you don't know how much this hurt me. Consider. Whatever you tossed is supposed to resemble a bird, and what bird ever came from your hand? So the average trainer takes Pup to field, has a pile of boat bumpers to side, reaches down and picks one up and gives it a toss. Well, that shouldn't be. Too many bad things happen with the handler-thrown dummy. For one, your arm is thrust forward in a vigorous manner. I don't want Pup to be spooked by this. I want you to be calm, placid, mellow—no sudden movements. I don't want Pup to shy away from you, to duck, to break his concentration because you've been abruptly physical with your body and arm. Understand?

You're always the pillar of Pup's repose, never someone who confuses or frightens him.

Same goes for those .22-blank-propelled shoulder guns (or hand guns) that shoot a dummy far afield. What bird ever flew out of your gun barrel on a day's hunt? None. Why should Pup be trained with something that never happens? Besides, there are two things wrong with those dummy launchers. One, they can impart an acrid gunpowder odor to the fired dummy and Pup can even blink the mark. Blink? Yes. That means Pup goes to the mark, sees it lying there, smells it lying there, but refuses to pick it up. Pup may even pretend not to have seen the thing and wander off in a mock hunt. This is very real and it can happen.

And two, Pup gets accustomed to seeing something fly out of a gun barrel—which is always associated with the sound of the shot. So it has come to pass that pups taken duck hunting the first time that have been trained with a dummy launcher rush behind the blind and retrieve the ejected shell—instead of going forth for the downed bird. Funny? Yes, in a way, but more sad than funny, and I don't want it happening to you.

So whenever possible, have someone else throw your dummies or your birds. Solicit the aid of your spouse, your kids, your neighbors—anybody. But get someone afield to be your bird boy. Out there is where Pup will see all his birds flush and rise, never from your hand or shoulder. When Pup's a seasoned performer, then do what you like. He'll know the difference. But don't throw your own dummies while training a young pup unless you absolutely have to.

Bird boy Boyd Hamilton tosses first retrieve for Butch Goodwin's Chesie pup at Glenwood Springs, Colorado.

Pup is off before dummy hits the ground.

Butch hurrahs him back in...

...and waits patiently to take the dummy.

HUNTING RETRIEVER CLUBS

America now has three hunting retriever clubs: The North American Hunting Retriever Association (NAHRA), the American Kennel Club's (AKC) Hunting Retriever Program and the Hunting Retriever Club (HRC) conducted under the auspices of the United Kennel Club (UKC). Talk to fellow retriever people and find out when these clubs meet for training sessions and test hunts in your area. Go there. Join. Attend their clinics. Train with them. They are the best sources of manpower and brain power to help you bring Pup along. For that's their sole and express purpose: for bona fide hunters to train and handle and test hunting retrievers.

Something else of extreme value about these clubs is that they conduct test hunts where no dog competes against another. Instead, all dogs run against par, which removes any bitterness from competition and keeps the club intact and cordial. Matter of fact, I hear many people say the hunting retriever club members are the only friends they have. A woman member of the Southern Arkansas Hunting Retriever Club who was having a baby found her club was the only group to throw her a baby shower.

These clubs set their own pace. The Arkansas members are so enthusiastic they meet before work in the morning, train most every weekend together, put on club hunts and help each other be prepared for the big circuit when it comes to their region so their dogs can vie for championship status.

Hunting retriever clubs are the best thing that ever happened to a retriever. Throw your support to them, participate, form your own club if there's none in your area, but by hook or crook get involved in their proceedings.

Should no one have information on these clubs in your area, then write: Hunting Retriever Club, 100 E. Killgore Rd., Kalamazoo, MI 49001; North American Hunting Retriever Association, PO Box 6, Garrisonville, VA 22463; American Kennel Club Hunting Retriever Program, 51 Madison Ave., New York, NY 10010. We'll talk in more detail about these clubs later on.

THE CATAPULT LAUNCHER

Should there be no one, or no club, in your area to help you teach Pup to fetch, then you still have another aid: a mechanical device. I'm talking about the catapult launcher, or bird thrower.

Let's examine the bird launcher. It's the most exotic piece of equipment I'll ever recommend you buy. You can find catapult launchers costing from $35 to $200. Naturally we'd all like to buy the lower-priced model, but there are reasons you should spring for the more expensive ones. The $35 job is a mechanical device, a mesh cage with a trampoline built in that's popped up by springs (thus launching the planted bird) either by depressing a trigger with your foot or by pulling a cord by hand.

The more expensive launchers are activated by an electrical impulse transmitted along an electric line that triggers an electro-mechanical switch, or a completely remote-controlled transmitter that activates the launcher by radio transmission.

There are some problems connected with the mechanical model. We reach down and pick up the cord, and in a matter of days Pup knows what's going to happen. We have to pull the cord to activate the spring. Well, we can help this along a bit. Saw off a three-foot section of a two-by-eight plank and mount that to the bottom of the launcher. Now anchor the plank with steel rods in the ground. Note your prevailing winds and lay out your trigger cord accordingly. Go get Pup and check cord (or heel) him into the bird's scent cone. Eureka, he's stopped immediately adjacent to the cord. But I repeat: To reach down and pick up the trigger cord will tell Pup the bird is coming up.

So we don't do that. We weighted the launcher and anchored it so we could place our foot next to Pup on the laid-out cord (the cord now being taut), and now we kick the cord with our other foot to activate the launcher. But you're right. Pup's not an idiot. He knows that when you kick, a bird is going to fly. So that's unnatural, too, isn't it?

As much as I want to save you money, those of you who can afford it should buy the remote-control launcher with the push button carried in your hand or hung on your belt.

But no matter what launcher you use, we can take all this a step further. Just at the end of the trigger cord you anchor a thirty-inch chain in the ground. You heel Pup to this spot and snap the chain to the D-ring of his flat collar. Now you have both hands free, the dog's chained fast, and you can pop out the planted bird and unsnap Pup to send him on a retrieve, or even fire a training pistol, then release Pup.

With remote control, however, the handler can place from one to four catapults in the field (now we're spending money) and trigger them up independently, thus giving Pup surprise marks in the beginning and multiple marks later in his development. And all of this without physically moving an arm or a leg.

There's a lot of equipment for sale to gun dog men that is useless or

Southern Arkansas Hunting Retriever Club keeps sausages smoking as some trainers run their dogs and others take a time-out for chow.

This is an electronic launcher that permits the handler more options than the mechanical model in catapulting a bird for Pup to mark down and fetch.

Professional hunting retriever trainer Omar Driskill tosses bird from sitting position and fires the gun, while holding Pup at side by anchoring his feet on six-foot check cord.

The slow-release launcher is built like a tunnel with a solid door in the rear and a gate opening in the front. Note hand (in photo) sticking through gate to introduce bird. We've intentionally left the wings open (which would be closed when loading bird) so viewer can see how mechanism operates when triggered.

at best has limited application. Some is even potentially dangerous. But the bird launcher is not included in these categories. The bird launcher is an aid that the isolated dog trainer (one who has no help) can't leave out of his program. Except for birds, the launcher is the best training aid the dog man's money can buy.

But I must admit, much as I hate to, that the seasoned gun dog trainer or the old pro can toss his birds himself and get good results. He sits on his dove stool with Pup heeled to side. Pup wears a six-foot, ⅜-inch training cord. And the handler throws the dummy to field, with Pup's trailing cord planted under his boot soles, then dramatically fires the gun (or in the beginning, makes the *pow* sound of firing with his mouth), releases the cord from beneath his feet and casts Pup for the mark. It can work. It does work. But it is unnatural and can never be an adequate substitute for a bird coming up from the faraway field.

But each of us must work with what we've got. We must improvise when we have to do so and grant that poor people have poor ways. The bottom line is getting Pup trained. Go about it however you can.

THE SLOW-RELEASE LAUNCHER

We start Pup's retriever training with a dummy. Only later will we switch to birds. In the old days we had to build our own dummies. We'd go to the fire stations and buy or beg sections of discarded canvas fire hose, then stuff the one-foot sections with cork or kapok (anything that would float and dry out fast). Then we'd either sew or staple the thing shut at each end, cut out a hole and fit the hole with a metal grommet. From this we'd hang a rope so we could more easily throw the thing. Or we could buy boat bumpers (that's where the bumper name came from) from a nautical supply house. Bumpers were used to hang over the gunwale so the hull of the boat wouldn't rub or bang against the adjacent dock.

Now you can buy dummies of every construction. Big ones, little ones, canvas, rubber, plastic. Some come in colors. Some are in the shape of a duck. Whatever turns you on. There are those who say dogs can't see orange, so orange ones are popular to make certain Pup uses his nose. I have no way of testing this, so I have no comment. I've seen dogs launch on water retrieves and keep raising up to look ahead to see the floating dummy. Yep, it was orange and they swam directly to it.

At a recent test hunt of the Hunting Retriever Club I witnessed the use of a new bird-release system manufactured and distributed by Winds, Wings, and Dogs, Inc., 2164 SE 14th, Loveland, CO 89537. This is a slow-release system: The bird is not lofted into the air, rather, the metal wings open slowly, not startling the game bird, and the result is both beneficial and surprising. (No, this device is not for dummies. But since I'm discussing launchers, this is a good time to present this equipment.)

The bird either sits in the opened box when the wings open or steps out and moseys about the near area. Which means the birds can be released ten to twenty-five yards in advance of the retriever's approach and be waiting in a natural state without being flipped in the air.

The slow-release launcher is triggered by a multiple-channel remote control that either hooks onto a belt, hangs from a lanyard, is carried in your left hand (for a right-handed gunner) or stowed in a jacket pocket. You dial the release box you want to trigger and press a button. Ideally you'd like at least three of these slow-release boxes in the field, but at a current price of about $360 each, you'd have to be a mighty dedicated trainer to fork over $1,000 for this gear.

The box is unexcelled for pheasant, quail and chukar, but pigeons will not hold upon release. They immediately flush no matter how slowly the mechanical wings open.

The slow-release system is of no use for us in puppy training. But later it is invaluable in teaching a dog a walkup. That is, check cording a retriever into a bird's scent cone to see game flush before the dog's nose and then you fire. Which is identical to what happens in a quail, woodcock, grouse, pheasant, prairie chicken, Hungarian partridge or chukar field on a typical day's hunt.

BACK TO RETRIEVING

You and Pup have been waiting months for this first retrieve, so let's get it right. Take Pup alone to some special place where the grass is cut or laid low: We want the dummy to be seen as it lies on the ground. Make sure there are no distractions, nothing to break Pup's concentration. Have no other dogs in the car since they'll bark. Find someplace where a motorcycle is not likely to go by or a plane to fly overhead. What we want is the quiet of an outdoor library.

Now let Pup smell the bird boy and all the dummies he's rubbed with his hands. That's the scent Pup will fetch. Then walk through the training field so Pup'll not be surprised by any distinct odors like a coyote bitch in heat that passed the night before. Also, some plants like alfalfa, for example, are tough for Pup to smell in. Then locate a casting line (downwind) from which you and Pup will work, and station the bird boy upwind—twenty feet distant is sufficient.

Serious trainers carry a tubful of dummies—each of which is smelled by Pup before training session.

Omar Driskill starts Pup off with bird boy tossing dummy and dog monitored close at side so Omar can grab him should he break.

Later the bird boy will fire a blank training pistol, but not now. We're doing everything possible to keep Pup from being gun-shy. Right now the bird boy will blow a duck call, all the while he's swinging the dummy about, and he'll throw it exactly where you've told him to. Note: It's easy for bird boys to miss the mark, even throw the blasted thing behind them. So have the boy practice while Pup's still in the car.

Only later will we use a bird catapult, if we have one, but for now we need the bird boy to keep Pup's attention afield and hype his excitement. Finally, you signal the bird boy to let the dummy fly and you release Pup for the fetch.

Here is where I've got to handle several different things at once. Bear with me.

If Pup is timid, reserved or confused, you need to let him break. We're going for boldness and spirit. No need demanding Pup to be steady for the cast. But should Pup prove staunch on the line—you say heel, sit, stay, and that's exactly what he does—then you can do one of several things.

In the old days we wanted to run our pups without a training lead. But in order to control him on the line, we'd thread a thin nylon cord through Pup's D-ring, bring the cord back to tie to our belt and then hold the off end in hand. If Pup stayed when the bird was launched, fine. But should he break (now we're talking about a spirited performer), we could either let him run free, releasing our handhold on the cord and letting it feed through the D-ring as Pup raced out, or we could hold the cord fast and jerk Pup down when he was, say, two feet before us (our cord is six feet long doubled back to make a three foot overall length). But we had to make sure Pup could take this kind of treatment and still strive to get the bird. Which meant then, and means now, you must know your pup, know what he needs, know what he can take and know how to bring him along. I can't help you there. It's up to you.

Professional trainers have used a twenty-foot check cord and let Pup get to the end only to be jerked rump-over-teacup. But that's not for us. We've done our yard work with the loose check cord, plus the power bar, and Pup has some foundation. Just a little suggestion should hold him.

Much, much later, if Pup should continue to break, the best method I've learned to keep him steady is to have two high-school football players stand behind the line. The bird flies, Pup bolts and the two roughnecks go berserk (in Pup's mind), hurling themselves forward, screaming (Pup cowers), mock-wrestling Pup to the ground and roughly wooling him. Then you step forward (you're always Pup's savior: calm, serene, mellow) and rescue him from these two maniacs who return to

Short slip-lead is attached to belt.

Cord is run through D-ring on Pup's wide leather collar and brought back to handler's grasp.

When Pup's proven steady to the thrown bird, handler commands back and lets slip-lead go.

stand behind the casting line. Now the bird flies and Pup glances back to see what those nuts are going to do. It's perfect for test hunts at hunting retriever clubs, for there's always a judge behind the casting line. Pup looks back and see this guy and says, "Oh-oh, there's one of those nuts!" He holds.

WHAT WE DO TODAY

In the past the classic field trial circuit determined the training program. Dogs were taught to play a nonhunting game where they had to lay their senses aside and operate within the will of the handler. They were robot dogs that were prided on how well they could deny their own instincts and follow a man's instructions.

But the new hunting retriever program demands the dog be freed to bring to bear all his natural senses and hunting genius. The dog's natural talent is more revered than his ability to hand over his self-will.

So all training duplicates a day's hunt afield. And having a dog run without lead—the classic field trial circuit prided a dog on ever being the subject of man's mental will—is no longer demanded. Now the dog is trained with a short lead, a six-foot lead, which is snapped to his collar and is dragged about with every exercise he does.

Our present stance is to be sitting on a dove stool with Pup heeled to side wearing his six-foot lead, which is clamped between the earth and our boot soles. The handler has a long gun that he does not fire in the beginning, and the distant bird boy who used to "Hurrah . . . hey, hey, hey . . ." is now vocally silent and instead blows a duck call. These are the primary changes in training. Then when the bird has been launched and landed, the handler *dramatically* extends the long gun in a shooting position and makes a *pow* with his mouth to simulate a shot going off. I emphasize the word "dramatically" since the man makes a weather vane of his body and gun—he makes a pointer for Pup to mark straight to the fallen bird.

SO NOW WE'RE READY

You've worked out all the details regarding Pup and you and the bird field and the bird boy and the wind. So you let her rip. The bird flies. And Pup sits. That's it. No response. No interest. Or he's confused and/or frightened. Oh my! Now you heel Pup out to the bird field and kick the dummy with your foot . . . let it fly. Possibly Pup will scamper after it. No? Well, we've got trouble. So now you get down on your knees, and taking the cord on the dummy, you scurry the dummy about on the ground—playing cat and mouse—enticing Pup. I see, he slinks away. Well, this probably isn't your pup, it's an older dog you've told the owner you'd try to work. So this is what you do.

Remember I told you it was easier to train thirty dogs than it is one. Well, it's the truth, and the truth is now. You need a chain gang.

THE CHAIN GANG

The chain gang is an extension of the litter-box check cord, i.e., other dogs train Pup. The pro will rig a chain gang that can accommodate up to twelve dogs. But you don't have twelve dogs. You may have only one. Which means you must talk your neighbors into lending you their Basset or Elkhound or English Setter. Generally, the retriever trainer ends up with at least three dogs. I once had twenty-nine.

Anyway, let's build a five-dog chain. To do that we'll need a length of stout, welded-link chain 38½ feet long. Fit each end with a large O-ring: We'll drive circus stakes through them to anchor the chain to the ground. Then every sixty-six inches we'll attach an eighteen-inch drop chain with swivel snaps at both ends. We want that sixty-six-inch separation to keep Pup from either fighting or being attacked by his neighboring dog. For I'll tell you, once Pup is put in this contraption he's going to shake, rattle and roll.

And the other dogs are going to resent it, for they're getting a terrific jerking on their collars, and sometimes all the dogs go berserk. But you're not there. Never can you be a part of anything bad that happens to Pup. Let him vent his rage or his grudge on others of his own kind. Once again, this device will teach Pup to give to the lead. So the chain gang has many purposes: to help teach all the basic commands, as well as to pep Pup up to want to fetch.

For what we're doing is the same as the football coach who makes the uninterested or errant player sit it out on the bench while he's forced to watch his team play ball. What an agony. Game after game he must sit there, until the need and desire to be on the field is so overwhelming, he foregoes his lackluster or indifferent ways (whatever it is that's disgusted the coach) and he begs to be let back in the game.

So we put our chain gang where Pup must watch other dogs fetch birds. Pay him no mind, for I can tell you he'll leap and splat over backward and scream and slobber and grow glass-eyed. Well, Pup brought it on himself: He wouldn't fetch the bird. So let him pay the price.

But let's say there are no other dogs. Well, that makes it tough for us but not impossible. Chain Pup to a stake with a short lead and leave him. Don't go around him except to deliver water or food and immediately take it away. Pup must know you're displeased. He must also learn that you're his only salvation, his only friend, his only refuge, his only pleasure. You are the only one who cares for him, so this heightens his care for you. This will translate into him wanting to please you, and come hell or high water he'll fetch up that dummy the next time it's thrown.

Now a dog can go thirty days without food. But he's got to have water every day (or every hour if it's hot) or soon perish. Water, then, is our ally. We take Pup water as many times a day as we feel it's important (or aids us in gaining compliance), and let him lap while we're indifferent. We don't say a thing or reveal any kindness in our expression or reach out and touch Pup. He's in solitary confinement, understand?

Enough days of this and you'll see Pup go wild when you appear. Depending on how you read Pup, either give in and release him or make Pup rough it out a few more days. You know Pup, I don't. It's up to you. But in the parlance of the rustic, "Pup'll soon let his milk down." He'll soon become biddable to your wishes.

Be mindful to always put your stakeout post or chain gang in the shade of trees; we don't want Pup passing out under a hot summer sun.

By training with water we have the opportunity to visit Pup many times a day. "But who's home," you say. "I'm at work." And you're right. That's why outdoorsmen need a good wife and no job. Outdoorswomen need the same thing. But I admit, I talk of the ideal. I also reveal in doing so why pros end up training so many dogs. The dog's owner just isn't available.

Anyway, you can go each hour and take Pup a drink. Of course he's not that thirsty. But your foreboding presence, your pretense of continued displeasure, has more opportunity to sink in. Because we're training with the power of the mind. Mind over matter. Mind over dog.

AGAIN, THE FETCH

We've got Pup back and he's rarin' to go. Great! Now the bird boy blows the duck call, displays the dummy and throws it to the short-grass field. Pup is cast into the wind, and though the dummy is in plain sight, Pup can't find it. So what does he do? He runs to the bird boy. It'll

Three birdy Labs and one hold-back Chesie test chain gang as handler displays bird for working dog to front.

happen every time. Well, that's bad enough, but something worse can happen. If the bird boy has a pile of dummies at his feet, he must get them picked up fast. If not, then Pup will have successfully switched birds, and this is a horrible fault while hunting or during a hunting retriever test.

The reason is this: One day Pup will be sent to fetch two ducks. One duck is dead, the other a strong cripple. You must get the cripple first or he can slink away. So Pup goes to him, the duck dives, Pup wheels about but can't find him, so then Pup bores toward the dead duck floating belly up. In the meantime the crippled duck gets away only to die in the tules, and now we've committed our worst sin against sportsmanship and nature: We failed to conserve game. And other than the love and joy we get from hunting and living with Pup, conserving game is the primary reason we have a retriever.

To avoid the possibility of Pup running to the bird boy, seed the area of the fall with several dummies (some trainers call this salting the area). Then the bird boy tosses one dummy into the scattered bounty. Now there's no way Pup can miss finding a bird. When Pup fetches it up, get on the come-in whistle immediately. Hurrah and wave your arms and whistle and get him coming to you, not heading for the bird boy. Kneel down if you must. Remember, Pup comes to you when you lower yourself.

Only it doesn't always work that way. That's because of another law of dogdom: *It's always easier to avoid a problem than it is to correct one.* Infinitely easier. For now we've seeded the bird field and Pup is picking up one dummy and dropping it only to pick up another. Again, Pup's switching birds. So you've got to go out there and kick the dummy you want fetched, and Pup will run to it and scoop it up, then you tell him heel and return him to the casting line.

But what do you do if Pup busts through the whole treasury of dummies and heads for the skyline? Now you lay on the sit whistle. Remember, one long blast. And you shout "NO!" If Pup keeps going, then get after him. And when you catch him, produce that plastic fly-swatter you've got hidden in the back between your tucked-in shirt and pants. Even swat Pup with it. We can't have a bolting dog. If that's going to be the case, then we'll have to run Pup on a twenty-foot check cord and stop him short if you see he's going to break through the bird field.

Or we can switch to birds. Pup'll stop for birds. But *birds* call for their own chapter, which you'll meet on down the line—or you can turn there now.

Something else Pup can do to both blow your plans and your mind is to pick up a dummy and run away with it. Once again that calls for running him on a check cord so you can milk him in. But when you tug on Pup, he sometimes drops the dummy, which then means we've got to go to the retrieving table—which is discussed in Chapter 6. There we make certain Pup never drops a bird. If your problem is that real, then go to the table now.

THE CAST

There was no need mentioning the physical act of casting Pup until I was sure you had him steady. You may even be down on your knees holding Pup at the casting line when the bird boy throws the bumper. But sooner or later Pup is going to settle and prove staunch on the line, and now, instead of just releasing him to go fetch, *we aim him.*

Primary to all this is Pup facing the right way and having his legs squarely beneath him. Carousel (circle) Pup about you and tell him to heel, sit, stay. Now lean back—you're sitting on your dove stool—and look down Pup's spine. Is he pointing toward that spot where the mark will land? If not, heel him again—guide him about you with his short lead, even stand up to do it, then sit back down. While sitting and carouseling Pup, you can use your nongun-side leg as an aid in aiming Pup. Extend the leg so Pup moves up beside it, yet doesn't crowd over it to be pointed wrong. If Pup's too far to front, or his front end is angled away, pat your outer leg with the palm of your hand and say, encouragingly, "Pup, heel." Or snap your fingers and order him back. He'll either scoot on his rump or spin around and recenter himself. If it's too far to rear, snap your fingers to bring him up.

But recognize this. Whatever way Pup's body is facing is the way he'll initially take off. The head controls the body, as witnessed by high divers and acrobats. As the head goes, so goes the body. So not only must Pup's body be facing the right direction, but his head as well. Granted, this is not so important in running marks, for Pup immediately adjusts upon the launch, but is very important when we get to running blind falls: that's sending Pup for a bird he never saw down. So work on this during mark training and you'll be far ahead by the time we get to blinds.

In the old days an American handler would place his flat hand (the way you reach out for a handshake) beside the dog's head. But now in America we see more and more handlers make a knife of their hand and place that knife directly above Pup's head, right between his eyes.

It matters not to me which way you do it, but I've had the most success with the hand beside the head. There's a reason for this. You must mesmerize the dog to aim him. Like a snake charmer, you get that hand going in tight circles, enticing Pup to focus, to concentrate. I call it waiting for the camera click. You can tell. When Pup slightly raises up, his neck stiffens, his head grows rigid to the neck, the eyes grow intent, the ears cock, Pup has the picture. So you snap the shutter by slicing your hand up like you were throwing a bowling ball and saying "Back."

In the hunting field where our primary interest lies, you can overhandle the dog all you want. But at a hunting test, you may be charged with lining a mark. I'll explain, even though lining comes later. Pup is expected to mark birds down and run to them more or less on his own. But Pup must be lined to a blind: that's a bird in the field Pup never saw fly or fall. Now we must really aim the dog.

Let's say we have a 100-yard blind. If Pup casts three inches to the left from your leg and maintains that misdirection, then he'll be three more inches off with each stride, which we can estimate at two yards. So by the time Pup reaches the blind, he's 150 inches off course, or 12½ feet. With any nose at all, he can wind the bird and fetch it up. But it doesn't always work that way. Pup can overrun the blind. Then you must handle him with hand signals and whistle commands back to the bird, and each whistle and each signal can be a demerit.

But I repeat: My interest is not having you and Pup place in a hunting test. My interest is the two of you going hunting, where game on the table is the goal and not a ribbon to put in a drawer. Yet I'll hastily add, once Pup hunts the way this book teaches, he'll place in any hunting test. *It's just that with Tarrant, the hunt comes first.* Dogs were hunting with man for time out of mind before anyone thought up a field test.

Also, I must hastily add that we would never let Pup extend his misdirection 100 yards. We would whistle him down and give him a cast to the right to put him back on line. I just use the above to emphasize a point. Okay?

Now let's jump back to the cast for a mark. Should Pup just not get the picture, then reheel him, carousel him about you once more and use your leg again to align him. Then lean back and check his spine and skull. Is he in line? Okay, then hypnotize him into focusing. It won't take long. Pup will catch on. He wants to succeed as much as you do, for he can't stand to break your heart. He can't stand your alienation. You're his world and there's no other. Like Gunner, Bill Berlat's Chesie, who wants to give Bill a hug. Gunner wants to love and be loved, and so does your retriever.

Omar Driskill's left hand is still extended as Pup reaches first of several in-line dummies for repeat fetching drill.

MULTIPLE MARKS

Sometime during 1965, I was judging a derby in Lincoln, Nebraska. Usually two birds taken on land, three more on water, then three more on land, and you've separated your entries. You'd have a winner. But this day a young pro had a string of miracle derby dogs who bingoed every bird down. It was getting dark, and I had to do something. So I asked for four birds down. Unheard of. But again, the dogs handled all four birds. Fortunately, some did it more easily than others, and I was able to close out the stake.

My point is this: Retrievers can be taught miraculous marking. Even at one to two years of age.

The average retriever handler is always confronted with a shortage of help. So he usually begins his multiple marks with what is called a "poor man's double." That's where one bird boy throws both marks. This can be quite unfortunate. The handler has his dog settled and motions for the bird boy to throw the first mark. The bird is lofted and falls. Then the bird boy turns 180 degrees and throws another mark. This can confuse Pup. He'll start to run for one but switch course in the middle of the field. Or he'll head for the right-hand bird, not be able to locate it, then race across field to fetch up the left-hand bird. And to make matters worse, Pup can stop midway and try to steal a bird out of the bird boy's dummy pile.

It is best if you have two bird boys for initial doubles. And have them throw opposite ways. That guarantees separation; you sure wouldn't want them throwing toward each other, now would you? And you want them to throw parallel to a line intersecting you and Pup. To throw at an angle would be confusing to Pup, for you'd be asking for intense discrimination in depth separation. So what we want is two birds straight out, in opposite directions, on the same line, thrown by two different bird boys.

There's hardly a pup that won't go for the last bird down. He'll scoop that one up and head back to your line, albeit he'll be looking sideways at the bird boy or even across field toward the other mark.

You're ready to receive the bird by having your angled leg pointing directly at the first bird down. Then when Pup walks about you, sits and waits for you to take the bird from his mouth, he's cocked on an exact line toward the waiting mark. And I don't want you to ever try to mark the exact spot of a bird down. You can't do it. Instead, mark a spot on the horizon where the bird fell. It may be a far silo, an indentation in a hedgerow, a distant, single tree. There'll always be something for you to point your nongun leg toward as Pup is making his way from the mark you've cast him to retrieve. I even slice a line in the dirt with the side sole of my boot. Then should I have to move about on the line to handle Pup to the first mark, I can glance down and see my scuffed line pointing toward the other mark.

CAN'T FIND THE BIRD

But what if Pup mismarks the bird? He's gone for the second bird down and can't find it, but to his credit he does not leave the area of the fall. Okay, have the bird boy help him. The boy walks over, hurrahing to Pup, then physically kicks the dummy high out of the grass with his foot, and Pup leaps to fetch and races back to the line. As he's returning, have the bird boy go fetch up the first bird down, for by this time Pup's forgotten where it is.

You can enhance Pup's performance by using the circle drill. Go to a mowed lawn and tell Pup to heel, sit, stay while you walk in a great wheel about him and drop a big stark-white dummy at each 90-degree angle to Pup. That's four dummies down in the circle. Then you return to Pup and carousel him about you, finally settling him to face one chosen dummy. Cast Pup. He'll go fetch the dummy you've aimed him for, while you situate yourself to create a launching pad with your nongun leg for the next dummy.

You might wonder at the value of the circle drill (or as it's sometimes called, "the wagon wheel"). Well, nothing builds success like success. If Pup gets to realizing that every time he's cast he's going to find the bird, then he won't panic when he mismarks and run aimlessly. Instead, he'll stick close to his notion of where the bird is and hunt intensely. He'll hunt precisely. Now when he's cast in heavy cover to find a dummy and mismarks it, Pup will stay close and hunt it up.

If Pup likes the circle drill, you can continually make it more difficult, seeding eight dummies, then even twelve or sixteen. Now Pup's really aiming off your leg and your hand. No way will he leave the area of the fall the next time he mismarks in high grass.

THE LINE DRILL

Another drill important to the hunter is the line drill. Here Pup is told to heel on a mowed-grass lawn, and the handler and Pup walk in a straight line while the handler keeps dropping dummies. Pup sees each one down. Then the handler walks Pup back past all the dummies, turns him around and sends him for the first one. Then the second, and so on.

Application of this drill to a day's hunt comes up when two birds fall as an over and under. That is, two birds drop in a straight line, one more distant from Pup than the other. Now you cast Pup for the first bird and he bingoes that one. But when you send him for the second bird, he gets hung up on the site of the old fall and won't drive further afield unless you put him there with whistle and hand signals.

Pup's fault is compounded should the second bird be a strong cripple that runs or swims away. Once again, we failed to conserve game. So that's why we have the line drill.

TRIPLE RETRIEVES

Finally there comes the day when Pup is sent for three birds. Once again we're confronted with a help problem. You really need three bird boys. But that's quite unlikely unless you're training with a hunting retriever club. So what we usually do is have one boy throw two birds in opposite directions, and then the handler throws a third bird a short distance from the line. I know! I said the handler should never throw the bird. And that is the ideal and that's what I wanted you to avoid—until now. But there are practicalities that limit ideals, right? Besides, by now Pup is no longer intimidated by the menace of your throwing arm. He is dummy-wise now and retrieving-wise. He knows your act of throwing is not one of hostility but just to entice him with a tossed dummy. But far better than this is to have one bird boy throw two birds and a second bird boy throw the third bird.

When Pup is far advanced on multiple marks, two men can stand opposite each other and alternately throw dummies while the other sends his retriever to fetch. There is only one dog. So dogman A throws the dummies and dogman B casts the dog for the retrieves. Then vice versa. Which means Pup is now working for a different handler. And this is good. This will be a time of proof. For Pup will be more inclined to goof off with a stranger. He'll be more likely to break, that's for sure, and even his marking can go to pot.

It is also important to always work an advanced dog from both sides, and when he does well, reward him on both sides. Pup's brain is split just like ours. When he's only worked from one side, the brain is only half-developed. We see this with horses where we can only mount from the left side. Such a horse was never trained for the right side, and this concept is important for Pup. What if the duck blind is situated where Pup's to your right instead of your left? You can think of other examples.

But back to multiple retrieves. . . .

HONORING

Honoring is very important, and very difficult, for a retriever. It means he must give up his frenzy to retrieve and sit there while another dog gets the fun. That is, he honors another dog's work.

Always start this with two handlers and two dogs. Each handler tells his dog to heel, sit, stay, but only one dog is going to work the field. Your Pup is going to sit at side compliantly, silently, patiently. Which means you've really got to anchor Pup. When you tell Pup to heel, sit, stay, you do it with emphasis. You even step out a ways and block Pup's view of the working dog. Later you can stand back. But to start with, you're going to need all the tie-downs you can conceive.

Then, when the other dog is finished working, he must honor Pup's work.

THE SERPENTINE DRILL

To teach honor, line up ten retrievers in a row. I know, you don't have ten retrievers; once again, join a hunting retriever club. Leave space between the sitting dogs where you can heel Pup behind the first one, in front of the second one, etc. Then you take Pup back to the start of the line and have a bird boy throw one bird afield (or in the water). Now you cast Pup for the bird while all other dogs must sit. Or you leave Pup, walk down the line and cast the fourth dog, or the sixth, or the tenth.

This is precisely the test given retrievers and English Springer Spaniels in Great Britain. All handlers walk their dogs at side when suddenly a pheasant launches, the gunners fire and the bird falls. But let's say the bird fell directly before the left-hand Springer (they're usually worked in pairs) or before the tenth retriever (they're always worked in a long line). Now you tell the right-hand Springer to fetch the bird up directly in front of his bracemate's nose. Or you tell retriever number one to run down the entire line of honoring dogs and fetch the bird up only to parade it back, rubbing it in (and they do), before each dog passed.

There are many dogs so full of spirit that they flatly refuse to honor.

By damn, there's a bird down and it's theirs, and they have every right to it, and they're going to fetch it, and if the other dog runs out there, they'll give him a thrashing. This is the type of performer that if you ever get a handle on him will really impress your hunting buddies and hunting test judges. But you'll die a thousand deaths over a lifetime wondering if he's going to stay for the mark, let alone stay to honor.

And this is a good time to mention whimpering. Test hunt judges don't want a noisy dog in contention. The reason is a noisy dog will interfere with another dog's work, plus he can disturb the hidden pheasant or the incoming duck. Well, what we have here is a dog so bird crazy he just can't control himself. And there's only one cure. That's tons of birds. I mean you shoot pigeon after pigeon, day after day, week after week. Remember River Oaks Corky? The miracle pup that spit up dimes to hold between his teeth to facilitate the fetch. Well, he won many national championships. But he didn't start out with that prospect.

You see, his derby trainer couldn't shut him up on line, so he sold him to a man with money who could afford 5,000 birds (birds are expensive if they're not self-trapped barnyard pigeons). Corky's new owner, Mike Flannery, of Denver, Colorado, would tell Corky "No noise" before each bird flew. And finally, with enough birds, Corky was able to contain himself.

But what both fascinates and amuses me is when Corky was eleven years old and the winningest field trial retriever of all time, Mike took him to the field trial line and forgot to say "No noise." And would you believe? When the first bird flew, Corky let out an awful whine. The gallery caved in with support. The old dog was still a bird dog, he was still a puppy, he was still filled with uncontrollable spirit.

In that regard some dogs are barkers, nonsense barkers, while others remain almost mute. Well, a chronic barker is a lifetime problem. This is one time you really have to get out the white flyswatter and use it. The display will shut the dog up momentarily, but a swat or two may keep him quiet for the rest of the day.

Should you have a barking kennel, there's three things I've done to get a night's sleep. Rig a pile of tin cans to a cord and stretch the cord to your bedroom window. When the dogs bark, drop the whole mess on the concrete kennel run. No, this is not for city dwellers.

Or get out there half-asleep and stumbling in the dark, then hose the pack down with water. Best of all is an electronic bark detector that triggers a shower placed over each kennel run, and when that water goes off, each dog scrambles for his doghouse. This costs money but can be worth it.

Mike Gould lines five Labs in a row, telling them "Heel, sit, stay."

The yellow Lab is called to Mike's heel, then serpentined through row of black Labs. This enforces staunchness and discipline in all dogs involved.

There are also antibark electronic collars you can outfit offending dogs with. They work. But the problem with them can be this: Once the collar is removed, the dog's barking again. Can you imagine the poor pooch having to wear the blasted thing the rest of his life?

Enough about noisy dogs. Just hope you never have one. I always said it was easier to get the missiles out of Cuba than to stop a noisy dog—and that's the truth of it.

THE REAL WORLD

Finally there comes the day when Pup's marks must be presented in the hunter's world. They'll be thrown behind hedgerows so Pup can see only the top arc of the throw. This will teach him to estimate trajectory and compensate for that difference between where Pup saw the dummy and where it landed. Other dummies will be presented in high cover, higher than Pup's head, so he'll learn to self-orient and overcome the handicap. Some will land in ditches that Pup will overrun. These will teach him to really mark close when birds fall. Some will be directly into the wind to teach Pup to use his nose, others with the wind so he'll sharpen his eye, and some will be presented crosswind so Pup'll learn to always swerve a little and hunt into the wind.

A dog with a terrific nose can be a detriment. I remember running Ch. Renegade Pepe in a Monroe, Louisiana, cotton field: It was set up for irrigation and each row was bordered by a deep ditch. We were running a blind (more about this later) where Pepe was sent to fetch a bird he saw neither fly nor fall. This full-bored-nose retriever would leap each mound (all the time smelling the distant bird) and hunt out the depression over and over. I had flown 800 miles to compete, for I was looking for a final point to qualify for the national running, and with each ditch I saw my hopes for that year's classic swirl down the drain. Pepe just had too much nose.

Other birds will be thrown for Pup on the side of a hill. It is a fact that dogs cannot hold a straight line at an angle up a hill: They always drift down. As they do on water (more about this later) when asked to swim directly into the wind: They crab to side.

Other birds will be thrown in sharp milo stubble to increase Pup's boldness. Any other setting you can think of to throw Pup off his game and work through will make a better retriever of him. But that'll not be easy with the Pup you and I are training. Remember? We spent all those days Happy Timing, where Pup's world disappeared so he could concentrate only on birds. Now you see why dog training is like links in a chain: One link must proceed the other, and on and on. Leave out a link and you have a broken chain. Or shirk your responsibility and end up with one weak link, and the chain can break at the most crucial time.

But the real nemesis for Pup is water. It's time we got wet, so here we go.

5

Water

THERE'S SELDOM BEEN A PUP brought completely through hunting retriever training without a problem. And after training several hundred retrievers, I can tell you that problem is usually connected with water. I've been known to answer letters to the editor sent to *Field & Stream* by writing, "In Pup's mind all water can be viewed as the Bermuda Triangle. Ships, planes and dogs that retrieve have all been lost there."

For water is spooky. And water is an obstacle. Consider: Most animals can swim, but when surprised at a water hole, do they not flee on land? Seldom do they leap in and try swimming to safety.

And not all water is created equal. There's stinking swamp water redolent with sticky muck, and high-banked creeks with submerged rocks and stubble, wind-lashed water, and water with strong currents poses unique obstacles, as do giant stands of clacking tules, or ponds clogged with beaver dams, or even water under a shadow. Do you know ducks don't want to swim through shadows on water? Water is just a mystery to all living things—except fish, huh? And who's ever interviewed a fish? They, too, may have some reservations about water.

But when Pup swims in water his head is close to the surface and he can't see as well as on land. He must protect his nose and mouth from getting slushed, and he must be able to shrug off getting tangled in brush or a long decoy anchor cord. Water can just be a den of horrors.

If you'll just realize that Pup would rather go by land than by water, you'll be way ahead of conquering this element. Later, Pup can enjoy being at sea, but should you force him in at the start, he'll always regard water grudgingly. And that's an honest fact. Remember it.

So how do we take Pup to water? On a hot summer day with lots of other dogs (or pups), in warm water with no cover and no high wind. That's the ideal and that's what you find. Remember, Pup was first introduced to water through Happy Timing. He ran with all the other dogs on a hot day and when they went into the water to cool their bellies and lap, Pup walked right in. So he went to water with no thought of what it was doing. He wasn't forced there.

I recently saw a satisfying example of this nonchalance around water, training hunting retrievers with the Southern Arkansas Hunting Retriever Club. National Football League tackle look-alike Jeff Devazier was there with his ten-week-old Chesie bitch pup Tyler, an absolute doll. She would stalk the bank waiting for the older dogs to bring in bumpers, and then she'd leap to water and swim out to try and grab the rope hanging to the dummy so she could steal the retrieve. She was dauntless, and Jeff, a professional hunting retriever trainer from storied duck land Stuttgart, Arkansas, has her started right.

All of which decries my warning of dread around water—yes, it can be a happy experience for a pup.

But what happens when it's no longer a game and you're sending Pup to water, instead of his entering on his own accord? The best way I've found is to put on your bathing suit, or waders, and enter the water yourself. That's what Jeff did. Pups, like Tyler, will automatically follow you. But don't go any deeper than wading depth for Pup. Let him have his feet on the lake bottom. Then play with Pup. Not to splash him, but to run and laugh and fall down (maybe), and let Pup know you love water, so why shouldn't Pup? Children are especially good with this. I recall kids floating in inner tubes where Pup voluntarily cast himself to sea so he could frolic with them. And he would paddle and try to catch them and they'd giggle and splash about and Pup would have no sense of peril. Just fun.

THE FIRST WATER MARK

When a retriever man says "running water," he doesn't mean there's a current in the stream; instead he means that Pup can "run in the water." Pup doesn't have to swim. That's what we want for the first retrieves for one special reason. When Pup is learning to swim in water (and many must, it doesn't always come naturally), he's inclined to raise his head so water won't splash his face, but this elevates his shoulders and in turn lifts his front legs up out of the water so the paws really do splash excessively now. This makes Pup raise his head even more, to the extent he's standing upright in the water. When this happens, Pup's tail, which usually serves as his rudder, is completely submerged and useless, so now Pup goes about in circles, he can't get anywhere, he can't hold a straight line, so now he panics and beats the water even harder.

Should Pup suffer this ordeal, there are a couple of things you can do. Toss a heavy dummy that will lower Pup's head in the water and thus automatically lift his rear end, then keep a slight tension on a check cord to reel Pup in. Or take Pup to water so much—and you accompany him—that he naturally learns to swim just as you did as a child. You can also press down on the back of his neck while he's swimming, which will elevate his rump, and everything will turn smooth.

But please remember this: Running water is noisy. So Pup cannot hear your whistle or verbal commands. And slapping water, white-capped water, water in a high gale or ocean water with a rushing tide can be very noisy, so Pup can't hear what you're signaling. Remember this—it's very important.

Now it sometimes happens in life that to take two steps forward you've got to take one step back. We've got Pup steady, he's not breaking on land marks and that's great. But when going to water, we want Pup to have all the spirit that's in him. Consequently, here's where we let Pup break if that's what he wants to do. To yell no, and jerk him down with his trailing six-foot cord in front of water could really work against us. Pup can assume you yelled no to keep him from entering water. Now what a mess! So never say no to Pup while on the bank and before entering water. It just isn't done until Pup's much older and can understand why you're yelling no.

Ideally you'll like a bird boy out in a boat or standing in water offshore. Then you walk Pup out on a peninsula and work him standing or on your dove stool. Later we'll work out of a blind. For we're always duplicating a day's hunt afield with our training.

Now there's a reason for the peninsula. Should Pup shy from water, he'll run the bank and this can be a serious fault. You'll see many a water-shy dog refuse a cast and spin about sideways on the casting line and run the shore, whining because he can't reach the floating dummy. Never let Pup have such a chance of bank running. On a peninsula he has nowhere to go but water: water to the left of him, water to the right of him, and water to the front of him.

In this photo everything is ideal for Pup's first water mark. Handler has walked Pup to the end of a peninsula, bird boy works from boat and dummy is thrown to land straight out from the peninsula so no angles are involved for Pup's water entry.

Also, when Pup spins about with the dummy in his mouth on a water retrieve, he'll automatically look for the nearest land to beach. Let that land be the peninsula where you're standing. When we get to multiple water marks, having the dog come directly back with the retrieve cuts down on time, so in the real world a strong cripple yet to be fetched might not escape.

Our first mark must be an absolutely controlled fall: no wind blowing the water's surface, no current in the water, no vegetation to hide the dummy or tangle Pup's legs while running (he's not swimming, remember?).

Tell the bird boy to blow his duck call, get Pup's attention, display the dummy, then toss it to sea. If Pup breaks, great! If not, really ram him on the cast. By that I mean, don't simply stick your hand out and say "Back." But thrust your arm forward with great vigor—be a launching pad like a sling on a jet aircraft carrier—and get Pup waterborne with a loud command. Not loud enough to startle him so he stops and turns around, but loud enough to propel him out.

Then be silent while Pup works. But when he finally does take the dummy to mouth and spins around so the water is slung from his tail, really put it on, "Hey, Pup, atta boy, whatta great guy, come on, Pup, hey, hey, hey." Clap your hands and, most importantly, position yourself immediately next to the water. For when Pup touches dry land, he's inclined to shake, and when doing so, it's easy for Pup to drop the dummy. Or worse yet, actually spit it out. Should this happen, don't reach down and pick up the dummy. Instead, kick it back into the water. Pup'll leap about and lunge to water to retrieve the dummy. On the next retrieve you must be fast and get it to hand before Pup drops it again. Never, never, never permit Pup to drop a dummy upon reaching shore. Why?

Our axiom is to conserve game, right? So Pup has fetched a stunned duck that's been revived during the retrieve. Pup spits the duck out on the bank and the duck flies away. Now you're without dinner, and the duck is going somewhere to die in the mud and the thicket. Uselessly. So always get the bird to hand, never miss. But should you just have a dog that won't hold the bird, then you'll have to go to the retrieving table, which comes up shortly.

There you'll teach Pup the command "Hold," while he retrieves. Then when you're on water you can repeat this command over and over while he's nearing shore. That way you can have a bird brought to hand.

ADVANCED WATER SINGLES

Stay with the peninsula launching pad until you're sick of it and Pup has it by rote. Pup never misses, there's nothing to it. Now you can move on. But in an instance when I discuss time spent on any one drill, I'd say *you should stay four times longer than you think you should*. The primary problem I've learned that confronts and defeats so many amateur handlers is the hurry in which they work. They don't take the time to really drill in the lesson they're trying to teach. I understand, you want a finished dog in five minutes, but it doesn't work that way. Five months won't be time enough. It takes years to achieve the all-age performer. In reality, Pup's learning faster than you ever could. Remember? What were you good at when you were six months old? A year? Two years? Give Pup time.

I repeat here what I said up front. Never reach out and grab at a dummy or bird—and never pull once the dummy is in hand. Instead, push. Push the bird in to wrinkle the back of Pup's lip so Pup will want to spit the bird out. Should you ever have a sticky-mouthed or clamp-mouthed dog, you can do one of two things. One, reach over and hook your index finger in Pup's off-flank and raise him off the ground. The nerves will prompt Pup to cough up the bird. Or two, get down and blow abruptly and forcefully into Pup's nose. This smothers Pup momentarily and he'll give you the bird so he can take a quick breath.

You can further achieve a bird given to hand by twisting the dummy or bird as you shove it into Pup's mouth. The teeth will slip, especially on a dummy, and Pup'll release the bird.

So that's the sequence on any retrieve: Push and twist so Pup'll cough the bird up. The most amusing incident happened with Ch. Renegade Pepe and me at an open field trial. Pepe was sent to retrieve one of two land blinds (he had not seen the birds fly or fall). But the birds had been used for marks and were badly shot up. So when Pepe, who was always sticky-mouthed, returned to the line, I casually reached over (I wasn't thinking) and pulled on the bird. Whereupon I got a thigh, a wing and part of a side. I handed this back to the bird boy and then reached over to take to hand the remainder of the mangled carcass. I then handed this section out.

At which point one of the two judges (they were both old and I fear approaching senility) shouted out, "Plant the birds," which is the command given to hidden bird boys to run out and place new blinds. But the other judge demanded, "What do you mean . . . he's still to fetch the second bird." And the first judge countered, "He's already done it . . . didn't you see him hand the bird boy [this person assists on the casting line] the second bird?"

The error was mine. The judges were Keystone Kops but I had forgotten to push and twist in taking Pepe's bird to hand. I caused the confusion, even though a befuddled judge contributed to the farce.

THE STRAIGHT BANK

Once the peninsula mark is ingrained in Pup, then go to a straight shoreline to have the water dummy presented. Continue to have the bird boy out in the water. I'm not ready for you to cast anything from land. There's too much chance Pup'll run down to the bird boy who threw the dummy and then launch to sea from there. Which means he ran the bank.

Now here you give Pup both short and long retrieves, and for the first time you cast him not only from the water's edge but back as far as thirty yards. When Pup's proven he's got intense water love, then and only then can you have the birds lofted from shoreline. By then Pup's hitting the water hard, striving straight for the mark, spinning about with great force and swimming directly back to the exact spot he entered.

When this comes to pass, tell the bird boy on shore to retire. That is, he actually hides while Pup's making his way to the bird. Then when Pup turns about he'll see only you and have no other person as a distraction. Otherwise, he might head for the bird boy with the fetch, and we don't want this.

Later, when Pup's proficient in the straight shore line test with all its variances, you can have the bird boy hold his ground. Tell him to be motionless and silent while Pup's working. We want no distractions.

During all these single water marks, make certain the opposite bank is not closer to Pup's point to retrieve than your own shoreline. Even advanced retrievers are prone to head for the nearest landfall.

Plus, should Pup start lagging on water retrieves or show any distaste for what he's being asked to do, then sweeten him up between water marks. Toss the dummy inland, let Pup run on dry land and scoop up the dummy to bring to hand, then shove the side of his face in the tall grass, shake rainbows of water crystals in the air and just feel good all over.

Remember, sound carries on water, so heed echoes. They can confuse Pup and cause him to head in the wrong direction in response to your whistle or vocal commands.

I was once hunting ducks on my farm pond when I fired at an incoming flight of green-winged teal. But the sound bounced back off the concrete dam and spooked a wad of Canadian geese to flight—pushing them from the cover they had sought at the dam to fly straight toward the gun. That's how confusing sound can be on water.

Always end every water session with Pup by giving him a treat. That is, let him romp and play, let him know he did good, let him know you're happy with him. Never put Pup away sad. It's like some married

One way to get Pup to drive straight forward on a single retrieve—and working a straight bank —is to place him in a retrieving line at a hunting retriever club. He'll be so hyped up to make the retrieve once his name is called, he'll not think of running sideways but plunge straight forward.

couples who say they'll never go to bed mad at each other. Get everything patched up in the field so Pup won't brood at home.

You do this by playing with the dummy, dangling it in the air to have Pup leap for it, or toss it high and close by for Pup to catch the way some dogs catch a thrown ball. Dogs love this and really appreciate your taking time to play this game with them.

DOUBLE WATER RETRIEVES

The primary problems with water can be twofold: one, the dog may refuse to take a cast, or two, he runs the bank. These are serious faults, and we do everything to deny they're ever happening. So when we start double water retrieves, we return to our peninsula. For Pup to blow out to the left (for a right-handed gunner) will just see him confronted with surrounding water. For Pup to try stopping at the shoreline and veering right, he'll be faced with another expanse of sea. So no matter what Pup does, right or wrong, he's going to get wet. For if his problem is a cast refusal, then you just walk into the water with Pup at heel. Now he's completely surrounded by water. You tell him to cast and he'll likely go. He's already wet.

Pup is performing for us out of a bond of love. One of the world's most noted retriever trainers once told me that a retriever would enter the water, for as bad as it could be, it wasn't as bad as staying ashore and suffering the consequences of the trainer's harsh displeasure. I don't want a whip-run dog, and I won't help you train one. If you and I can't be bright enough to motivate performance, then let's go rope goats or race frogs or do something where a dog doesn't defeat us. For that's another ironclad rule of dog training: *When pup makes you mad, he's defeated you.* Never forget this. Anytime you have an impulse to strike or kick or electrically shock Pup, suddenly recall: You've just let the dog have the upper hand. You just let the dog force you to lose control. And if you can't control yourself, how are you going to control (what is incorrectly called) a dumb beast?

So Pup is psyched to water, never beat to go there. The beating won't work anyway. Oh, Pup'll fetch water marks, but now you've built a robot dog. One that works to avoid terror, not one that performs for love and bonding and good feelings. Brutality can build a mechanical dog, but intimacy builds a companion that performs to keep the faith.

Now all water problems should have been worked out during Happy

Timing with other dogs, or children, taking Pup to water. But if there's some lingering doubts or fears in Pup's mind, then you have to dispel them. Enter water yourself and leave Pup ashore. Entice him to you with tidbits. Feed him, walk with him, pet him, reassure him with voice, then throw the dummy (in play) for Pup to romp after and fetch. Reward him with food again. Keep it up until *the water disappears.* You'd like for water to be a pleasure for Pup, but if you can't have that then at least try to make water neutral. Make it disappear.

You can also take Pup out in a boat and toss dummies for him, but note, a lightweight boat scoots sideways in the water when Pup leaps. So this may further frighten him. *That's why you first work Pup out of the boat on land, then take the boat to water.* Also, when bringing Pup aboard an extraslender boat, lean to the offside as Pup boards on the near side, and then come back to center along with him and you're both balanced. If the boat has some width, you can help Pup board by reaching out and grabbing his coat, or letting Pup get his fronts legs over the gunwale and then pressing down on the back of his neck.

As with singles, the ideal is to have water doubles tossed by bird boys in the water. If you can't afford two, then have one boy throw a poor man's double. As with all initial dummies, they should be thrown at a 90-degree angle to Pup: straight out from the bird boy and parallel with the casting line where you and Pup sit or stand. Recall: Dog's have poor depth perception. Only later can dummies be angled toward, or away, from the shore.

Another aid to Pup for these first double retrieves is to have the bird boy close, say ten to twenty feet from shore. You signal when to throw each bird by raising your arm opposite to Pup. As always, he'll retrieve the last bird thrown. Of course we've chosen a windless day (so the dummy won't move), in water with no current and no cover. Again, this is running water. Cast Pup and meet him at shore so he can't drop the dummy when he shakes. Heel Pup about you, tell him to sit, then cast him for the first dummy down. Again, meet him at shore.

Also—that dummy Pup just gave to you—throw it far behind you on the peninsula so Pup won't be tempted to drop the dummy he's carrying and pick up the one he just handed you. In other words, we think ahead and do all we can to help Pup get it right. Later it doesn't matter. But in building the foundation it's thousands of times simpler to avoid a problem than try to correct one. Usually the only way to work out a problem is to return to basics, and that sets your training program back several months.

TRIPLE RETRIEVES

Balance is what we seek as retriever trainers. Not too strict. Not too lenient. And for your sake, don't make it all too complicated and precise. I recall a friend who had a skin cancer removed, and the doctor (a good ol' Texas boy) told him, "Treat it with neglect." In other words, don't worry so much about the consequences, don't baby it, don't piddle with it.

So that's one side of the coin we should honor. Yet the other side tells us to be correct about what we're doing and simplify it in Pup's mind as much as we can. I've written hundreds of gun-dog training columns, many training books and thousands of letters in response to readers who wanted to know this or that about what I wrote. Two things became evident to me. One, I am a dog trainer who took up writing and I had to make myself clear, I had to be a good writer. But at the same time, the man or woman who buys the book must have equal dedication and skill: *He or she must be a good reader.* Not only for the words in the lines, but for the words between the lines.

What I'm leading up to is this. Among those thousands of letters I received, three training faults became obvious. I've already mentioned one: Trainers go too fast. But the second failing is that trainers make things too complicated—and writing with precision and giving ultimatums as I do, I can see how that would result. The trainers were (and are) too rigid, too demanding, too serious. Relax, have fun with what you're doing, for Pup can read your mind: Make it all uptight and sober and he'll tense. The third training fault is that handlers don't stick to links in the chain: They don't put link B into link A, and link C into B, and D into C and so on.

Here's how that happens. We are training Pup on water retrieves and at no time have we introduced the decoy, which can be a real distraction to Pup. Yet a man with a partially trained retriever might want him to fetch opening day of the waterfowl season and *whamo,* there they are: the decoys.

We've also not mentioned firing a long gun or what to do if Pup refuses to retrieve or hold the retrieve. Nor have we discussed working out of a blind or quartering for upland birds and so on. Well, this is the Tarrant system of training and I've put these links together so many times I've learned what works best. Not just for me, but for everybody. And that's why we have the sequence presented in this book. But none of this would work for you, let's say, if Pup refused to fetch. In that case you'd have to jump ahead to the retrieving table (See Chapter 6). So it's up to you to know what's best: to know your pup and know your capabilities as a trainer.

Now here we go to triple water retrieves. Well, that's no big thing. If Pup can mark doubles he can make triples. But there has to be some orderly process in our training, and so multiple birds fall into different subcategories. Also, it's time to introduce the gun.

HANDLING A GUN

The new program of training and testing hunting retrievers has grown so big and so fast that manufacturers have not kept pace with adequate and needed equipment. What we must have is a blank shotgun shell of *moderate noise*. But all that's available on today's market is a manufactured .12 gauge popper (a blank shell) made for the classic field trial circuit where gunners are generally far distant from handler and dog. Consequently, these poppers are made excessively loud. But hunting retriever training and some test formats call for blank shells to be fired by the handler with *dog to side*. Which means the sound of these blank shells is overbearing to the dog, literally driving him to earth.

Now I speak here of two poppers: the standard .12 gauge shotgun blank shell (which is too loud), and the .22 short training pistol blank shell (which is not loud enough).

When something is not available, enterprising people improvise. And what they do is not always advisable for others to try. Some professionals use the cheapest live loads they can buy. *But here you must have very controlled training grounds and training personnel*—you can't have someone shot with live ammo! If every training round is going to be live ammo, the handler should really be alone; and if you are going to use live ammo, being alone is what I recommend.

Other trainers hand-load their own poppers with some recipe a colleague has given them. *But beware. These hand-loaded poppers can fail to thrust the wad through the gun barrel. Consequently, you fire a second popper and the wad strikes the clogged wad and the barrel can explode. I absolutely do not recommend hand-loaded poppers.*

Or other trainers say, "Oh, what the heck," and they use the excessively loud factory popper. *The result being induced hearing loss for both man and dog, plus a real chance the dog can become gun-shy. So I do not recommend these poppers be used, either.*

So what's left to us? The .22 blank training pistol shell. But the short blank won't feed in all .22 rifles (and that's what we want) for

Omar Driskill works an American water spaniel on birds with poppers. Bird boy to front and off-camera launches bird, Omar fires and spaniel is sent for retrieve. This is the new method of training Pup, for he eventually will learn to mark off the gun: an imperative for the new hunting retriever.

continuous training. And then I discovered that many trainers were using the power tool *long* .22 blank because it would feed. Yet right on the label it tells you this shell is not to be used in sporting arms. *So, no way can I recommend the trainer use these hand-tool loads for training. Never can you use a product contrary to the manufacturer's recommended usage and applicable instructions.*

So what does that leave us? The blank .22 shell with the short cartridge suitable for a pistol. And that's not what the hunting retriever trainers require, for as you'll see they must out of necessity *have a long gun.*

In all my research I found but one ray of hope. In talking with Winchester Arms, Dave Trowbridge, assistant production manager, told me his company was sensitive to sportsmens' needs and, since I had made those needs known, would immediately start testing a long star-crimped .22 blank load similar to power tool loads (which would both feed and give us enough noise). And if that extensive testing shows that such a product would be safe to use as a general-purpose *noise* blank, then Winchester will plan to introduce that product for general consumer use.

Also, Winchester has the tooling for a .410 blank cartridge, and if enough people would contact them affirmatively for both the new .22 blank and the .410 blank, they'd certainly try to manufacture them.

Write Dave Trowbridge, Product Management, Olin Corporation, Winchester Division, 327 N. Shamrock St., East Alton, IL 62024.

Until then I have no alternative but to recommend you do the following. We're training hunting retrievers and we hunt with a gun. And we must train the way we hunt, and hunt the way we train. So the gun becomes an everyday, every dog necessity. But we have no satisfactory blank shell for our guns.

Let me explain. The benefits of training with a long gun in hand are tremendous. First you "shoot" the bird thrown right (let's say) with the long gun, and then to get the bird thrown left, you must cross over, extend your body before—or even up against—the seated dog (remember, you're on a dove stool) and thus physically move the dog so he faces the thrown bird and marks down the barrel.

Your aiming is done slowly and dramatically, plus you stay low so the dog practically looks down the barrel with you. In the accompanying photo you'll see that Omar Driskill has all the flowing extension and intensity of a vintage automobile radiator ornament. No one ever said flair couldn't help you train a dog.

So what are we to do? *All right, here are my recommendations.* Use a .12 gauge pump or double-barreled shotgun shooting manufactured poppers, and keep your shooting to a minimum for the dog's sake. Most of the time you'll be aiming the gun, getting low and on line with the dog's head so he marks down the barrel, and you'll say *Pow!* Other times you'll shoot the excessively loud poppers.

Or use a standard .22 blank training pistol and extend the right arm full length to "shoot" the right-hand bird, then pass the pistol to your left hand and "shoot" the left-hand bird—keeping the left arm straight and extended and no higher than the level of Pup's head, making your arm and training pistol a substitute long gun.

Now to review: *At all times you must follow manufacturers' recommendations for the use of their respective products. At no time should you train with a live load with others about or with a hand-loaded popper, nor use blank .22 shells in guns where their use is expressly forbidden.*

Of course you'll use live loads while actually hunting afield. But the ultimate law of gun dog training is this: You can never be too busy hunting to take the necessary time to train your dog. Which means this is when Pup will be trained using live ammo.

Now a word about the hunting retriever clubs and their use of guns. At the time of this writing, the Hunting Retriever Club is the only club that permits the handler to shoot poppers on some tests. The North American Hunting Retriever Association permits the handler to point an unloaded gun (no popper in the chamber, nothing), and the American Kennel Club does not permit the handler to touch a gun whatsoever.

Since the Hunting Retriever Club does have the dog handler shoot a popper, and wads propelled from such shells can be injurious, each judge is required to pass his own state's hunting safety course. I don't care if he's hunted sixty years, he must have passed that course. It would be well advised for all hunting retriever trainers to do the same thing. So the Hunting Retriever Club not only exists to train hunting retrievers but also to teach and practice proper gun safety. Unsafe handling of a gun at a test hunt can cause ejection from the event by a judge.

Remember: A loaded gun (live shell or popper) is serious business, never forget it. The consequences can be deadly. And please force yourself into this regimen when using a shotgun: Always keep the gun on safety and always keep the breach open. I cannot emphasize gun safety enough. It must be second nature and it must be absolute to you and every gun in your hand. You have a device that can maim or kill dog and human (live load or blank): Respect that, remember that, go to every precaution to avoid that. Please!

Also, in the following pages whenever I use the term "long gun,"

Omar really streches it out to give working dog a long view of the gun barrel. In this case the dog seems calm, but Omar is mighty intense. But that's the way he trains: committed.

I'm speaking either of the shotgun with or without a popper, or a training pistol presented with an extended arm.

And since this is the first time I've mentioned a gun in training, I want you to skip now to Chapter 10 to learn how to handle a gun around Pup, and how to introduce the report of a gun to him so we don't have a gun-shy dog. This is very important. Turn there now. *And for you and your dog's sake, write to Dave Trowbridge at Winchester.*

BACK TO MULTIPLE MARKS

In the beginning the bird boy blows a duck call, then throws the bird and shoots it with a blank pistol at the height of its arc. Pup soon learns this routine, so he can pull your leg by running or swimming to the gunner and checking off to find the bird.

If this happens with water triples and you're not on a peninsula, this assures us of the likelihood Pup's going to run the bank, and when he gets to the gunner, he'll turn rapidly and dive from shore. *And we cannot have a bank-running dog.*

Consequently, if a bird is thrown wrong—bird boys are not always accurate—and a bird lands close to shore, say at a 45-degree angle to Pup, then Pup has the desire to run the bank and leap out to fetch the dummy. Can't be. So you short-circuit Pup's thinking, have him heel, walk him along the shore, carousel him about you, sit him facing the bird (which is now straight out) and cast him. Never, never, never let Pup run the bank.

Two reasons. Some befuddled hunting test judges may ask for this in a test. Damn the man or woman who does. Oh, incidentally, let me butt in here. We make a real mistake calling judges judges. They should be called helpers. Then they wouldn't be so inclined to foul up retrievers at test hunts or trials by asking them to perform *faults* to place. At no time can a judge ask a dog to make a mistake to make a win. Horrible! Call them helpers and they'd think differently about what they're doing. Called judges they're inclined to hurt, not help. Okay, as I was saying before truth broke in, never let Pup run a bank in training and he won't run one in a test hunt. And two, it's the same old thing we've discussed before. Pup marks the bird from the casting line. He has that angle. But now he turns and runs down the bank, takes a 90-degree entry and leaps to water. His original mark, his original line to that mark, is shot. He's no longer marking the bird, he's hunting a blind. For on this test the dummy landed in heavy cover and Pup can't see it. And now he swims amuck, just frothing the water, knocking down the cover.

Advanced water retrieves can take many forms. Here's a good drill. Man in boat amidst decoys and sticks. Pup must really mark and not veer from line going for fetch.

Eventually Pup must also work from a blind on water. Here two gunners wait for bird boy in boat to launch a mark while Chesie cheats and walks out of duck blind door.

So here's what we do on a bank runner.

Water can be a den of horrors for a retriever, so many pros advise you never, never, never say no to Pup around water. If he's got a bad water entry, let him go. For to say no when Pup's heading for water is telling him *not to enter the water,* and that's the big problem we can have. Water refusal. Well, we can correct water refusal by going to water ourselves and coaxing Pup in. I once made an amateur field champion out of a black Lab I bought at two years of age that would not enter water on a blind. I stood in the water and fed him, then threw dummies ashore that he fetched to bring back to water for tidbits. There are ways. But correcting a bank runner can be the hardest of cures to achieve.

There have been pros who hid helpers along the bank who leaped out and grabbed the bank runner and beat him or actually shot him with bird shot. Or one enterprising pro festooned a log with tin cans and lofted the log up in a tree, and when the dog ran the bank, the pro dropped the contraption to frighten Pup, but instead it all landed on the dog's back. Almost killed him.

So if you should ever see Pup leave the casting line to run the bank, shout no and mean it. This will drop Pup's anchor. Then tell him to heel, get him back to you and walk him either to the shoreline where he should enter or even into the water. Now cast him. This way Pup knows you're not telling him to avoid water, for you walk near it, or into it, with Pup at side.

If that doesn't work, then run Pup where there's a steep-cut bank to his left—so he can't leap out sideways. Or pile debris there, or situate yourself next to heavy foliage.

Or if none of this works, you'll want to go to blind retrieve training and get Pup skilled in the looking glass drill. That'll stop your bank-running problems.

SWITCHING BIRDS

There's not much problem with switching birds on water. But it can happen, especially if one dummy enters heavy cover, Pup can't find it, so he leaves the area and hunts elsewhere. Or a distant dummy floats into the area where Pup is hunting. The reason Pup's not so inclined to switch birds in water is this: It's not easy to swim. It takes great effort and it takes a long time. Just once I'd like for you to go to sea with Pup (and wear chest waders). Get close enough to Pup to feel the kick of his legs as he pushes himself about. He'll nearly knock you over. And if you're in a bathing suit he can slice your leg open with his back-stroking paws.

Also, if Pup starts marking off gunners (or birds boys) and runs to them only to take a 90-degree turn to the bird, then have the gunners and bird boys "retire." That's a term that means the helpers actually hide. They throw the bird and Pup automatically looks for the next bird. As he does so, the initial bird boy and gunner drop behind cover or into a ditch or behind tree trunks. Now when Pup looks for them, there's no one there. That'll break Pup of thinking their presence will help him.

And there's another fault that happens more likely on water than on land. And we might as well handle it here.

THE POP

Pup "pops." And you may rightfully ask, "What on earth is that?" That's a field trial term that means Pup casts for a mark or a blind retrieve but en route stops his quest and turns about to you for help. Admittedly this comes up more after the dog is taught to handle, but it can also happen with a young, started dog.

The way we correct a popper is to turn our back on him. He's asking for help, so we ignore him. Better this all comes about on land where it can be worked out without the dog associating your alienation with the water he's treading. Matter of fact, take him to land and hope he does pop. For now we get to correction.

This is a humane training book: We train with intimacy, not intimidation. But there comes a time for Pup the same as it came for us. Dad or Mom more than likely lowered the boom. And this is how we do it.

On land we yell Pup down, get him to sit, or cower, and we go to him, to the exact spot he popped, then physically reach out and grab him on each side of his neck and lift him from the ground to vigorously shake him. For man, horse or dog: Once you've taken their feet away from them, you've defeated them. We hold Pup with his head immediately before our face, and we tell him in no uncertain terms exactly what we think of him. Then we put him back on the ground, tell him to heel, sit, stay, then we walk back to the casting line and, holding our casting arm high, yell "Back," and throw the arm forward.

If Pup won't take the arm cast, then go to where he's sitting and wheel him about to face the old mark (or intended blind) and cast him. If he still won't go, then bring him back to the casting line and have the bird boy throw another dummy in the exact spot the first one landed (or was hidden).

If Pup pulls your leg again, then not only do you go to him and physically pick him up and shake him, but you then put him on the ground (on his back) and mock maul him, shouting all the time.

But when it's all over and Pup's finally got the dummy that caused him so much trouble, then sweeten him up with a couple of fun retrieves and clapping and hurrahing and carrying on. We never put a rebuked dog away. We always stow him with cheer in his heart.

You can see why this handler response is more readily carried out on land than sea. But that doesn't mean you can't go to Pup in water (for he will test you there, too) and give him a mauling and a shouting and a slam down in the briny. Then standing right there in the water, give him a cast to the dummy and yell "Back."

If you don't have the strength to lift the dog, then tackle him, knocking him down, and mock maul him. He'll get the idea. For we're training like mama-dog. All bark and no bite: all mock malice.

Then, too, there's always the white plastic flyswatter. It can perform miracles.

And one final thing. Many dogs pop because they've received too much training pressure. They predict failure and correction so they turn for help. If this is the case, then take the dog out of training for a week or two and bring him back gently. As you handle this dog, do not nag. Keep everything upbeat. Okay?

HIKING A LEG

Male dogs are compelled to mark their territory. Or some dogs (both male and female) can be chronic wetters. And this cuts down on class, to say nothing about efficiency, when fetching birds. Some dogs will even stop to move their bowels. And that's not their fault. It's the result of not exercising a dog properly before it is taken to the casting line. It is so easy to take care of this, so don't ever let this become a reflection of your management.

Well, there's not much you can do about it but say no, and if the dog is returning with the retrieve, yell "Heel!" But if he stops to relieve himself on the way out, then you've got real problems. This means his hunting intensity is not high enough to overcome any desire to eliminate or mark the territory—an unforgivable fault. Nothing must stop or distract a retriever from fetching his mark or blind. Nothing!

Another thing you can do if you see Pup stopping for a "potty break" on the retrieve is to get on the suck-in whistle, coaxing Pup with your dropped and flagging arm to get on in. It's a matter of reading your dog—you'll catch on—and maybe the judges won't if you're in competition.

If this behavior afield becomes chronic, discipline your dog the same way as for the popper. Mock maul Pup. But you must know that for some males this territory marking is not even on a mental level. It is rote. It is mechanical. And it is compulsory.

Going straight to live birds will help curb "pit stops" afield. The birds will stoke Pup's fire to drive all the way to and from them without stopping. Stopping to relieve himself is acceptable as the dog is coming in so long as he doesn't drop the bird. Another thing you can do is carry a spare bird in your hunting coat pocket. When you see Pup slow down, roll the bird out and let it fly away. That'll get Pup running toward you.

THE KNOW-IT-ALL PUP

There's a final fault on marking we must discuss. That's the dog that gets so field-wise that he notes the first set of gunners (or bird boy) and just as they fire and throw, Pup turns his head to look for the second set of guns. In other words, he leads the action all the way around the field. Now this can't be. If Pup starts this, then tell the second bird boy not to throw his dummy but instead yell "Back!" and cast Pup for the one bird down.

This will startle him. He expected more and nonchalantly turned to the next bird. Now he's told to get the bird he refused to mark down. Well, Pup will probably amaze you. Dogs have terrific peripheral vision: They have 250 to 270 degrees of vision where we have but 180 degrees. They can see more in movement out of the side of their eye that I sometimes think I can see straight on.

But keep doing this "interrupt" drill until Pup mends his ways and watches each bird all the way down.

THE TRUTH ABOUT WATER

Seasoned waterfowl hunters and wise test-hunt judges know that if Pup's going to fail it will usually be in water. There is just a reluctance in some retrievers to go to sea. That's why you really pep them up on their way to the duck blind, be that to hunt or to pass a test. Leave all your worries at home: no money to pay taxes, your company is relocating, your daughter just dyed her hair orange. Leave it all behind. For if not, Pup can sense it and it'll put Pup off just when we must have Pup up for water.

Of course many dogs love the water, and other dogs—once they're wet—forego their reluctance. But a poor water performer will usually take his reluctance, or his obstinacy, to his grave. Remember the two-year-old I saved in water and made a champion? When he was fourteen, he cheated on a blind retrieve, went a half-mile out of his way on his return and crossed a bridge rather than swim back. This water thing is always in their mind once they've had a problem with it. For Pup's sake, have no problems in or around water.

6

The Magic Table

EVERY GUN DOG, natural retriever or not, must be compelled to retrieve. "Oh no," you say, "my dog does it all and I never had to force him in any way." That's great. And maybe he can go through life faultless this way. But what do you do if he quits you? Nothing. That's what. For you've built no foundation to work from, to correct from. That's why we have the magic table.

Traditionally, the term for what we do in this chapter has been called "force breaking" a dog to retrieve. I resent the word "force" and discard it. The term grew up in a time when hands-on training was all handlers knew. But we're training hands-off. Remember?

Like most training techniques the beginnings are lost in antiquity, but a David Sanborn of Mississippi was using the rudiments of what we teach on bird dogs in the 1880s. E. M. Shelley (1874–1959) of Columbus, Mississippi, possibly America's greatest bird dog trainer, refined the process. Then Delmar Smith of Edmond, Oklahoma, ten-time national Brittany field trial winner, brought the technique to fruition. I presented it to the world in a 1977 training book, and since then young innovators all over America have further refined the system.

What's involved is this. The dog is elevated on a table and snapped to a rigid cable between two upright steel posts. Pain is then induced so the dog will open his mouth in vocal protest and a hard dowel is placed between his teeth, and the dog is told to fetch. He holds the dowel until you tell him to leave it or spit it out or give it, or whatever command you favor.

Now that's a simple overview for a simple process, but explaining in detail how it's done appears to be complicated. Bear with me and make every effort to get it right. More trainers become confused with this technique than almost any other. And again, it's the same old problem. The trainer tries to go too fast. Stay with the table longer than you'd ever expect. Don't think the dog's got it, *know* the dog's got it. And realize you're not finished until Pup does all you ask of him on the magic table—*and his tail is wagging.*

THE BIRD

I've intentionally avoided birds, for they are magic themselves. *You must realize the birds can solve almost any problem Pup ever has.* Bird dog is Pup's generic name, and bird is the first half, the important half. You can't train Pup without a bird any more than you can train a football quarterback without a football. Now I assume you've tried some birds with Pup on his dummy drills, and you've kept up your Happy Timing, and Pup's confronted many a flyaway bird in the wild. But you and I have not discussed birds: their importance, their maintenance and their use. I'd like to do that, plus the magic table, all at the same time—but alas, that's impossible. So I've chosen the table first, even though we will use birds here. But I don't want this table bird to be Pup's first bird contact. I want that to have been a thing of joy afield. So depending on how you and Pup are getting along, turn to Chapter 7 now, and then come back here if Pup's never been around a bird or if he seems bird-shy. Okay? We'll wait for you.

THE NO-ALTERNATIVE RETRIEVE

In the beginning, as with most dog training, man was barbaric. I've said it before: "Man's inhumanity against life." Man forced dogs and horses and cattle and everything else to do his bidding. But no living thing can be successfully forced to do anything. There is always rebellion in its mind. Plus, forced behavior is always lackluster. And forced training begets a berserk animal once it's liberated to use its own wits.

In the beginning of history man got down on the ground and did one of several things to get Pup to open his mouth for a fetch. He grasped

112

Pup's nose and mouth in hand and dug his thumbs between Pup's clenched teeth, then inserted a dowel, or buck (more about these later). The problem with this technique was twofold: 1) The man was off-balance and cramped kneeled down like that. This made him conducive to losing his temper. And 2) Pup was manhandled. He wasn't brought along by the head, but by the hand. And it was heavy-handed and *Pup knew it.* He could see the man strained before him, he could feel the man's hands prying open his jaws.

Then man started grabbing one of Pup's paws and squeezing it to get Pup to open his mouth. Still later man pinched an ear. I even know one man who became a pro who broke a dog's shoulder by trying to apply a half nelson wrestling hold. There has been no end to man's lunacy or his barbarism.

Later the dog was elevated on a table so the man could stand relaxed and balanced. This was a significant improvement—as was the nerve hitch. The nerve hitch was made by wrapping a string about the two center toes of one of Pup's paws and pulling the string to trigger a nerve that prompted Pup to open his mouth in protest. It was perfect. There was no physical damage, and more important, no imprint. Release the string and the nerve pain died instantly with no scar tissue.

And even more important to our way of thinking and training, the handler was not touching the dog. He was holding a string at least a yard away. Of course the dog knew the man held the string, dogs are not idiots, but the dog did not feel the warmth of the man's hand. And that's vital to us. The dog knew the string was hurting him and the man held the string, but the offender (the man) had now removed himself one step (the string) away from the dog.

Later on—and this probably will not have much application to you—handlers found they could work several dogs on the table all at the same time more easily and more effectively then they could work one. But there again, where are you, as an amateur, going to get all those dogs?

STEP BY STEP

First order of business is to build our magic table. Gather some lumber and do two things: 1) Make the table very sturdy, and 2) Make it waist-high—no more, no less. This will center the average retriever on the table so that when you present the dowel with your right arm bent at 90 degrees, the dowel will be exactly mouth-high on the dog. And why 90 degrees? So you're always comfortable, everything natural, your arm bent without tension.

Author has seen magic tables take myriad forms. This one is all wood with a wood brace running between uprights so they won't collapse inward. In every case, you have a table built for stoutness, a cable with swivel snaps and two upright posts.

If a dog balks or fights you, then double-tie him. Run a loop about his flank plus hook a rope or chain to his collar. Make sure the collar cord is left long so Pup can reach for buck when nerve hitch is pulled.

You can use two-by-two or four-by-four legs with a marine-plywood top. Brace it all for strength, and make the table at least three feet wide and six feet long; but I'll tell you now, the longer you make the table, the better. I've seen some pros—now that this technique has caught on—making tables thirty-six feet long.

Centered at each end of the table we'll drive in steel posts of channel, rod or pipe (some pros use wood posts) to which we'll attach two turnbuckles and a cable thirty inches above the table. The cable stretches across the entire length of the table. We tighten the cable banjo-string taut with the two turnbuckles. Now you can either put an O-ring on the cable before you attach it to the two turnbuckles, or you can wait and clip a swivel snap there. We want something free and easy to run up and down the cable. Soap the cable for lubrication if you have any friction.

When we place a retriever on the table, we'll have enough lengths of stout chain, or enough swivel snaps snapped together, so the dog sits naturally with no slack between his plain flat collar with the stout D-ring and the cable. Each dog is custom-fitted.

Now look about your garage or barn and cut off nine-inch segments of the last garden tool handle that broke, be that hickory or oak. We want dense, hard wood for these dowels. We don't want Pup to comfortably bite down and indent this wood: We're fighting hardmouth, okay?

We're almost ready to put Pup on the table, but there's one last piece of equipment we need, and that's a three-foot long section of ⅛-inch nylon cord. Are you ready?

THE DEAL PUP CAN'T REFUSE

Get Pup, put him on the table and attach his collar's D-ring to the swivel snap hanging from the taut cable. Let Pup settle, don't rush anything. You've just taken Pup's legs away from him—that's why vets put patients on a high, slick steel-topped table. They immediately render the dog helpless. If Pup wants to stand, sniff and walk about pulling the swivel snap or O-ring along the cable, fine!

Now outfit yourself with a good pair of thick, but pliable, leather work gloves. When Pup's settled, go to him and put your left hand (if you're right-handed) over Pup's muzzle, your fingers prying open his jaws. Insert one of the oak dowels, groom Pup's lips so they aren't pinched and stand there, holding the dowel in Pup's mouth, saying over and over to the dog, "Hold, hold, hold."

Then tell Pup to "Leave it," or "Give," or whatever command you use, and push the dowel into Pup's jaws as you twist. The dowel will immediately be spit out.

Now there's a way to situate the dowel in Pup's mouth. Put a pencil crosswise in your own mouth. Too far back and you gag, but let the pencil come forward to rest just behind your canine teeth and you're comfortable. You could hold the pencil all day. So this is where we center the dowel in Pup's mouth.

Now once Pup's taken the dowel, you remove your left hand from his muzzle and place all four of your fingers under the flat collar beneath Pup's neck. This leaves your thumb free to raise up and press into the V of Pup's jaw, which insures he holds the dowel. Your right hand, during this time, is placed over Pup's muzzle and is grooming his lips to make sure they aren't pinched, stroking his face and caressing his ear.

The hand is ever ready to grab the dowel should Pup fight, squirm, fishtail, leap, lunge, duck (yes, he can do all these things) and the dowel comes free.

Keep putting Pup on the table and introducing the dowel until Pup gives in. That may be the first session, that may be the fifth. You can help this along by grabbing Pup's lower jaw with your left gloved hand and just holding him fast, waiting for Pup to sigh. He'll usually try you three times, then give up.

But let's say he doesn't. You've got a big, strong Lab with a mind of his own. Or a Chesie that has just sworn death to you and all your kind. Okay, get a card table and shove it into the corner of your garage. On the right-hand wall attach two O-rings eighteen inches above the tabletop and two feet from each other. Now use a short piece of cord and tie Pup's collar to the front ring. Use a longer piece of cord and loop it about Pup's waist. Now he's secure. He can lunge but a little bit, he can't rear back, he can't jump sideways, he can't sit, he's stationary.

Now go through the process we just tried above. Keep doing it until Pup says, "Okay, you got me," and the fight's all done. This will come to pass, just persevere.

Or you can throw a second rope over your taut cable and cinch it around Pup's waist. You get the same result as the cornered card table.

THE NERVE HITCH

The table, the leather collar, the O-ring, the swivel snap are all just hardware. The genius of the whole system is the three-foot section of ⅛-inch nylon cord: the nerve hitch.

Attach a nerve hitch by circling Pup's leg just above carpal joint with nylon cord.

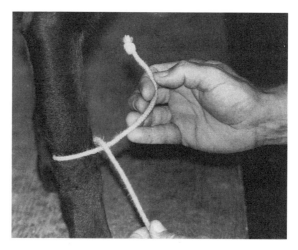

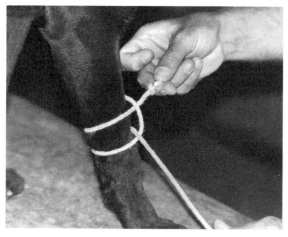

The cord is then tied in a clove hitch with the end hanging down.

The cord is then laced between Pup's two center toes on his left foot (for a right-handed gunner). The cord is pulled with the left hand while the right hand introduces the dowel.

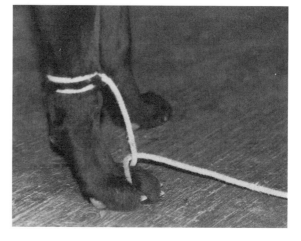

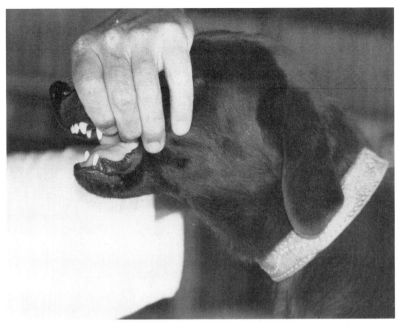

First, with no nerve hitch attached, Pup's mouth is opened by handler compressing hinge of the jaw.

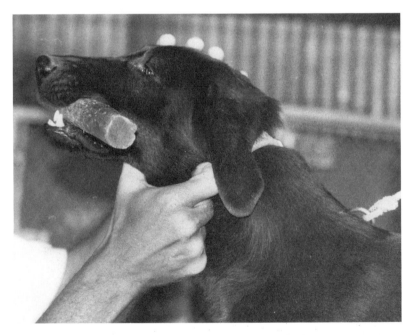

Dowel is then inserted and Pup is told to "Hold it."

We've now returned to the retrieving table and Pup stands snapped to the taut cable before us. So we go to him and tie the cord on his right front leg, if you're right-handed, just above his carpal joint—that's what we call the knee in the dog's front leg—with a clove hitch knot. Adjust the clove hitch so the cord hangs straight down over Pup's right foot. Now slip the cord around the two center toes of Pup's right foot and tie a half hitch. Shove the knot up tight against Pup's foot: The trailing end of the cord lies on top of Pup's toes and hangs from the table.

Here we go!

Present the dowel before Pup's mouth with your right hand. Say fetch as you pull the cord with your left hand (and gradually intensify the pressure) on the nerve hitch cord. Pup will soon open his mouth to say "ouch," as you immediately place the dowel in his mouth, *while at the same time you release pressure on the cord.* You just flat drop it. The sequence then is: presentation of the dowel, the command fetch, the pull on the cord, the mouth opens, the dowel's inserted and the cord's dropped. It all happens in less than a second once the mouth is opened.

Now you groom Pup's mouth, make sure the lips aren't pinched, locate the dowel immediately behind his canine teeth, and to insure his holding the dowel, you say "Hold," and the left hand is placed in the leather collar with the thumb thrust up into the V of Pup's jaw.

Have Pup hold the dowel no more than five to ten seconds, then say "Give," or "Leave it," and both push forward and twist the dowel at the same time. When all this is finished, really praise Pup and even walk him up and down the table. Let him relax. Then repeat the process over and over. Finally, you'll let the dowel stay for a minute just to make a point.

Now while all this is going on, you are also prepared should Pup spit out the dowel. You have two or three more dowels in your right-hand rear pocket. With a fast draw you present another dowel, while the first one clatters to the floor, and once again you pull the nerve hitch that is always handy—it hangs over the lip of the retrieving table.

Our verbal sequence is "Fetch," "Hold" and "Leave." Emphasis is placed on the "Hold." This is what we say over and over as Pup is returning from a water retrieve so he won't stop at the bank, shake and spit the bird or dummy out.

A FIGHTING PUP

Now all this time Pup may not be standing placidly before us. He may be fighting, ladies and gentlemen, he's top-seeded on the main event

Finally, nerve hitch is attached and handler pulls cord while he presents dowel before Pup's face.

Once Pup accepts the dowel, release the nerve hitch cord (Gould has not released it here but has relieved all tension) and insure Pup holds the dowel by placing your right hand under his chin with fingers through collar and thumb poking up into V of Pup's jaw.

and he's giving it everything he's got. He's rearing and twisting and leaping and lunging and dropping to the tabletop. He's creating a terrible commotion. And if it's too much for you to handle—then go back to the garage. Start your first retrieves on the card table with the two wall anchors. Or throw a waist cord over the cable.

I know it's messy business and it's the only time I'll ever ask you to inflict pain on Pup, but this is one time it is imperative we do so. Pup is a retriever and what value is he if he can't be guaranteed to retrieve? And the only way that can be accomplished is on this table. For what are the results? Let's say Pup's graduated from the table and he's just brought a dummy back to the line for you to take to hand, but you missed it. You tell him to fetch and he balks. Well, we've been working on his right leg, so we just tap that leg with our left boot. Bingo! The light goes on. Pup doesn't want back on that table, the stimulus to fetch has just been recalled and down goes his mouth—compulsively—to fetch up the dropped bumper.

Or you can run Pup with the cord tied to his carpal joint—*but not between his toes*. Should he sully up on you and refuse to fetch, just reach down and pull the cord. The cord doesn't have to be around Pup's toes; the light comes on for him and Pup will be eager to get the dummy or the bird.

So I repeat: With the natural retriever, there's nothing you can do to gain a guaranteed retrieve, but a dog that's graduated from the magic table is unlikely to ever let you down. Yet should he, you have recourse to mend his ways.

But we're not finished with the table; there's more work to do.

THE BUCK OR DUMMY

Now we take a dowel and drill two holes in each end, through which we insert four pegs and make what's called a buck. The pegs protrude at 45-degree angles to each other, and their benefit is to hold the dowel up from the table so Pup can more easily take the dowel to mouth. Note: Some trainers just use a dummy and don't make a buck, but these trainers are not fighting hardmouth. You want hard wood to mitigate against hardmouth.

We place the buck (or dummy) at the far end of our table and tell Pup "Fetch." Ideally, he'll run down the table, scoop up the buck, you tell him, "Come here," and he's just made his first table retrieve. Now see why some tables are thirty-six feet long? If Pup's reluctant to go, just reach up and grab the sequence of swivel snaps holding him to the cable and walk him down the table. Once you get to the buck, should Pup refuse to fetch, you pull the nerve hitch cord and demand he do so: He will!

Then you can leave two bucks down there, three bucks and so on, and just keep running Pup back and forth. Now it's all getting to be fun for both you and Pup, the pain and the fight and the struggle are behind you.

Next we introduce a dead, bloodless, frozen bird. We freeze the bird with the toenails tucked in, for they can be sharp and hurt Pup enough to cause a fetch refusal and even bird-shyness. That can't be allowed to happen. We get such a bird by putting him in a paper sack, sealing it and waiting for the bird to naturally go to sleep. And why a frozen bird? Well, we're still fighting hardmouth. Pup will be less inclined to bite down on a frozen bird than a thawed one.

Now we place the bird at the end of the table and send Pup to fetch it.

Then we take our entire sequence of one buck, to multiple bucks, to the frozen bird, to multiple frozen birds, to the ground. Pup's got his legs back and it's the moment of truth. If Pup proves to be a fail-safe performer, he may never have to see the table again as long as he lives. If Pup has any problems, it's back to the table until he gets it right.

THE BENEFITS

So what have we gained through all this? Plenty. Let's just look at what happened. Pup entered a crisis and came out of it a stellar performer. This bolds him up. Why? Because he sees how pleased you are, which further builds his confidence. The magic table does all this. It makes fighters give in and the meek stick their chest out. Pros now know all this can be supported by putting other dogs on the table with Pup. There is uncanny communication between dogs. They are "talking" all the time. How they do it is beyond me, but they are constantly checking in with each other. And they take support from each other. One in crisis will cause a rush of adrenaline in another, and all dogs try harder.

It's the same with settling. One dog remains placid and he can cool down the lot. So one dog's in panic while working, but he sees his bracemate unaffected. Makes him wonder. It can even make him more receptive to the handler's desires.

But more than this . . .

Pup races length of table to fetch buck. But heed this! You don't get to this advanced stage until after many days on the magic table with the nerve hitch.

Pup's progress on the magic table can be enhanced by working other dogs with him. Here two handlers work three dogs. The significance: Dogs take heart and gain confidence through "communication" among themselves.

Should you send Pup for a mark or a blind and he can't find either, he'll not leave the area. He knows he's been commanded to fetch (that means the same as "Back"), and he's compelled to get something in his mouth no matter what. That's why Pepe once brought the bird crate full of birds back to the casting line because the cock pheasant shot for him had run away. I still get tears of laughter in my eyes each time I see him in my mind: coming backward, dragging that heavy crate, with all those screaming and flapping birds. It was the grandest of all things.

Later there'll be a third command that means the same as back and fetch, and that's "Dead bird." This is said after the quail have exploded, the guns barked and there's been deadfall. You walk Pup to the spot you saw a bird hit and tell him "Dead bird," or you can say "Fetch." I say both over and over. "Fetch it up, Pup, dead bird, dead, dead, deeeeee-aaaad." Pup won't leave the area. He's compelled to retrieve. The bird will come to hand and score another victory for conservation.

The magic table also furthers the bonding process between you and Pup. It's been something else you've got through, *successfully*, together. We see it in marriages. Travails, calamities, insurmountable troubles—and they're weathered—and the couples weld tight together. That's what happens with you and Pup.

Should Pup ever balk—let's say at water's edge—and refuse to take a cast, then tie the nerve hitch cord above the carpal joint (but not around the toes) and hold the end of the cord in your right hand (for a right-handed gunner), and as you say "Back," and thrust your left hand up, you also catch the cord in your left heel and kick that leg forward. The kick will tug on the joint and Pup'll jet out of there. Once again the light is dazzling.

A REVIEW

You know you've made a fail-safe performer when you hold the dowel six inches before Pup's nose, say "Fetch" and he lunges forward to take the dowel to mouth before you can even pull the nerve hitch cord.

Should Pup freeze on a dowel, remember to push and twist, plus also give a short, powerful blast of air up his nose. It's easy to do. The nose is right before you. Or, if Pup still balks, reach over and lift that flap of skin before his hind leg with a finger. This prompts Pup to drop the bird.

Always afield, should Pup quit you, all you have to do is tap that right leg with your boot. This will remind him of the consequences and he'll hop to it.

I've even carried the nerve hitch cord in my hunting coat pocket, and should an errant performer surface, I merely had to dangle the cord before him. He knew what it was and did he get to work.

We took our sequence from single dowel to multiple bucks. Then we introduced the frozen bird. Finally, many frozen birds were seeded at the end of the table for Pup to fetch. Then the whole thing was taken to earth, Pup had his legs back and we held our breath to see what happened.

Finally, we went on to dummies and freshly killed birds. Now Pup could handle the hot scent and not bite down. For not only are we building a never-fail retriever, we're also doing away with hardmouth, sticky mouth and dropping the bird on fetch.

We worked on all these as the days went by, and Pup graduated. Or maybe we had to stay weeks. It all depends on you and Pup, doesn't it?

But finally it all worked out and Pup became the dog you always dreamed of, and you became the handler he would uproot trees and flatten thickets to get a bird for.

7

The Blind Retrieve

IF YOU think you and Pup have been through hell up till now, think again. This is where the fire and brimstone and the ultimate hallelujahs really come about. For here we're asking Pup to hand over his self-will to us and we have no magic table to enforce our desire.

For what we're doing is telling Pup we know there's a bird out there, and on blind faith he's got to fetch it up and he's not to use all his God-given senses to do this job. No! He's to pay attention to us and *we'll* direct him to the bird.

Now that's asking a lot, isn't it? For whether you realize it or not, Pup's aware of the fact he knows more about the outdoors than you do. For example, Pup knows he can wind a live bird better and faster than he can a dead one. Why? You mean you don't know? Well, he does. He smells the bird's breath. That's right. Plus, Pup hears the birds talking to each other and shuffling about in the cover. Didn't know that? Well, Pup knows it. And it goes on and on, and now you're going to be the big shot and take over and Pup has every right to scratch his head and wonder—if not balk.

Well, if we go about it right we can earn Pup's compliance and make it all fun. For nothing, absolutely nothing, can equal the exhilaration that comes from handling a dog over rough terrain or through a quagmire of a swamp to a downed bird—and do it all together. It takes team work and mutual understanding and mutual faith in the ability of the other. And it takes you to think ahead to help Pup and it takes Pup to do whatever he's told.

THE BASEBALL DIAMOND

There are successful pros and astute amateurs who have made a science of teaching retrievers to fetch up blinds. I, quite frankly, don't understand most of what they're talking about. But I'm not paid to be bright, just to love dogs and try and help others who feel the same way get the most out of their canine companions.

So no matter what's been thought up to date on teaching blind retrieves, nothing, and I mean nothing, works better than the simple, age-old baseball diamond.

You heel Pup to home plate then on out to the pitcher's mound, where you pile up some big, fat, stark-white dummies on a mowed-grass lawn. Pup can see the pile out there when you've returned him to the home plate. He's ready to go and you tell him softly "Line, line . . ." as you move your casting hand in tight circles, mesmerizing Pup to concentrate, and then you order with low voice "Back." Pup runs out there and grabs a dummy and heads back to you. It's all bliss and good times and nothin' to it.

Then you put the pile of dummies at second base, then at first base, then at third base, and each time you send Pup for the fetch and each time he happily complies. The fun's still holdin'. Incidentally, if Pup won't go, then just toss a dummy out there to hype him up.

But now the dummies are placed only at first base and Pup is told to heel facing the pitcher's mound. Pup won't want to do it. You'll have to work with him. Finally you get him zeroed in to run to the pitcher's mound by softly saying "Line" (more about the soft voice later), and Pup casts as you say "Back," and just as he passes the pitcher's mound, you hit the sit whistle. Remember, that's one long blast. Pup should come to a grinding halt, turn about, you whistle again and he sits. Then you wait for him to compose himself and, raising your right arm perpendicular to your body, you step in that direction and command "Over." Pup will probably just sit there. So you do it again. He still won't go, so you walk ever nearer to him, doing the same thing over and over. Stick out your right arm, walk that way and command "Over." Still he doesn't move.

But now you're immediately before him and you run through the casting sequence, the light goes on and Pup bolts over there to fetch the bumper. Then you run the test over. And over. And over.

In this photo Pup is worked on an athletic field: White line transversing photo is irrigation pipe. Dummies are seeded at first-, second- and third-base locations. Handler casts Pup toward second base, hits him with a stop whistle, Pup stops and turns to face handler, then handler gives back. Photo caught Pup twirling around to head for second base—he is not going to first.

Then you put the dummies at third base and run Pup toward the pitcher's mound only to stop and give him a left-hand over. Again you will probably have a hassle. But finally Pup'll get it.

Now the hard times begin.

You put piles of dummies at first, second and third base and run Pup toward second base only to hit him with the whistle and cast him toward first base, where he makes the retrieve. Then do it all over but cast Pup toward third base, where he makes the retrieve. And finally you hit him and stop him at the pitcher's mound, only to raise your hand straight up, palm facing Pup, and step forward as you command "Back." Pup will spin about, head on to second base, fetch up a dummy and return. You've got half the battle won.

Now you make everything more difficult. You cast Pup toward first base where there are no dummies, then give him a left-hand over to third base for his fetch. Or to second base. And then you find every combination you can think of to run. Next, you expand the baseball diamond. Make it twice as big, three times as big. Then you take your regular-sized diamond to a field of moderate cover and run your drill. Then heavy cover. Then through ditches and sheet water and roadways and hedgerows and thickets and whatever else you can find to foul Pup up.

And remember all this time: *As Pup gets more proficient at running blinds, his marking will go to pot.* It happens every time. So don't just concentrate on handling drills, but keep sending Pup for marks. All kinds of marks. And if he can't perform like he used to, understand. It'll all come back one day.

SPEAK EASY

Now why the soft voice? *A handler's voice must be equal to the distance of the dog afield and the situation in which the dog's placed himself.*

If you're loud on the casting line, then you've just shot your wad. There's nothing left to put Pup down when far afield.

Also, a loud voice commanding "Over" *will drive a dog back, not over.* But back! This causes a scalloping route on the way to the blind, especially in water.

Here's how it goes. The dog takes the initial cast to side, but the verbal blast of the command is overpowering and the voice drives Pup back. He's trying to comply with the arm signal to get over, but the voice prevails. So he makes a feint approach at going over, only to veer off and end up going back—the same wrong direction he was going before you whistled him down.

So you'll see many experienced handlers say nothing on an over. They'll just whistle Pup down, then step sideways with that arm raised and keep silent.

Or another handler who knows the characteristics of his dog may combine the over with a suck-in whistle. That's right. He's telling the dog to come in with the whistle and get over with the arm signal. The result is the dog will take the over. For sure, there's been nothing to force him back—which is the usual fault. And why is that? Well, Pup knows he has nothing in his mouth so he'll naturally prefer going back to find something to please you. He feels your calling him in means he's failed and you're going to play the heavy with him.

Consider another type of dog. He's so birdy you can't stop him from running back. You send him "Back" at the casting line and it's back he's going. So with this dog you can't give him an over, for at best he'll give you a combination of an over and a back—all at the same time. In other words, he'll run an oblique, or a 45-degree, back. Well, you know this about the dog, so you stop him short of the over you really want to give him, go ahead and give the over, and as he drifts back on the over, he comes out on the exact spot you intended for him to cover.

It's all called knowing your dog, reading your dog and handling him.

STAYING ON COURSE

Pup must learn to hold a line. It calls for a geometry wizard as a dog to get this done. For the line will cross a path in tall grass, and both Pup and we will veer toward the path of least resistance and he'll be enticed to bend his line. Well, that can't happen. That's why we run Pup in the early days where nothing has made a path. Nor is there a road or lane, not even tire tracks that have laid down the grass. Pup will want to run these natural corridors.

But what of ditches? They'll throw Pup off. Whatever lead foot hits first on the opposite bank—Pup will veer in that direction. As he'll also drop off the slope of a hill. So we crab him at the casting line. Aim him too far toward the top, knowing his natural fall will bring him out on the spot we intended him to hunt.

And while out hunting, a fence can even stop Pup dead in his tracks. That's why we teach him to jump. It's easy to do. Put a two-by-eight

A three-foot-high fence of hog wire topped with two strands of barbed wire would stop an ordinary dog in his tracks. But not Web. Here Gould holds down two strands of barbed wire while Web jumps the obstacle.

chunk of wood in a doorway. Call Pup to you. He'll naturally jump the eight inches. Now put two of these pieces of wood on top of each other. Pup is obliged to jump sixteen inches. Then place three of them and he must jump twenty-four inches. Finally, nail a rope to each side of a utility-room door out in the garage and drape it with gunnysacks or a painting sheet or an old tarp. Now call Pup to you and he'll leap the rope that is four feet high. And that's high enough to clear most fences in America.

Over in Great Britain they're great on jumping stone walls. But we don't have many stone walls in this country. We fence our pastures with barbed wire and we sure can't train on that to get Pup jumping.

There are aids to help us teach Pup to run a straight line. Find a level pasture of low grass and drive through it, all the while dropping dummies out the window. Then stop the car, get Pup out and cast him down the line of dummies. He finds the first dummy and returns, then the second and so on.

Or go to a school yard and get Pup flat up against the chain-link fencing. Seed dummies along the fence line. Cast Pup for each one. Or find a brick wall, or the long side of a factory building, anything to channel Pup on a straight line.

Incidentally, talking of using fences in training, this is a good time to mention the diversion mark. Pup is run out of a fence gate. He goes south of the fence to fetch a bird thrown, but as he's returning he sees you toss a bird on the north side of the fence. That's a diversion bird. Pup will want to go to that bird with the first bird still in his mouth. But no! He can't! This comes up on a duck hunt when Pup's making one retrieve, only to have you shoot another bird on his way in. He must always return first with the first shot bird.

But now one final lining drill before closing. Go to a school yard and get Pup flat up against a chain-link fence. Why flat up? Notice. When you cast Pup, his tendency might be to duck away from your arm as he leaves the casting line. Then usually the dog self-corrects, but not all do. If your dog does not, you must help him. Also, you must stop being so forceful in thrusting up your casting arm. So you get Pup pinched between you and the chain-link fence, and dummies seeded all along the line, and you cast him. Again he picks up each subsequent dummy in turn.

Omar Driskill wedges dog against fence to get a straight line. Still, dog kicks out as he runs fence, showing just how hard it is to run a straight line.

Handler places himself and Pup in gate. Pup is run to the north side to pick up a dummy thrown there, but as he's coming back with the retrieve, a dummy is thrown by another bird boy south of the fence. Pup can't switch birds: He can't get through fence.

PHILOSOPHY

There is something very important we must discuss. We're training hunting retrievers where all their natural instincts and innate genius are enhanced to bring about a successful day's hunt afield. Yet here we are taking away the dog's options, telling him exactly what to do afield—and this will prove even more true in water. Well, this is an outgrowth of the classic field trial circuit.

I want you to study the photo I present of a J-shaped peninsula heading into the water where it is separated from another identical J-shaped peninsula by a small stretch of water. Now, let's face it. A dog living in the wild, a coyote, a wolf, a fox would run down this J-shaped peninsula and dive into the water to fetch a crippled duck dropped between the two Js. And you as a hunter would probably walk your dog the length of the J-shaped peninsula, then cast him for the fetch.

But the classic field trial game *demanded the dog do all water work via water*. To touch land was to have failed the test. So the dog is sent all the way by water—even through the two Js to a duck landing in the distant body of water. Well, this philosophy has hung on in hunting retriever tests, which is not duplicating a day's hunt afield. So if you want a hunting retriever specifically for hunting, then walk him down the J. But if you ever intend to run Pup in a test hunt, you'll have to cast him to the downed bird all the way by water.

"How could you call this enhancing the dog's natural talent?" you might well ask. There is only one answer. The dog driven by water through brutality will do the job, but should he swim from sight and turn about and not see his handler, he'll go berserk. He does not take control of the situation, he does not have the ability to "take over" and fulfill the job. But a love-trained dog will know that once he's out of sight he's on his own. So he realizes you control all his actions on a blind, but he further knows that should his senses tell you you're wrong—or should he go from sight—then he's a free agent.

For example, let's say the duck located between the two Js floats to shore. Of course the dog winds this and heads for the fetch. But you're playing the old field trial game transferred to the new hunting tests, and you keep whistling him down and casting him back to the spot you marked the X: that place you saw the duck fall. Well, the dog trained with brutality will forego his senses and blindly follow your instructions, only to go to sea and fail the test.

But the love-trained dog will overrule you and, taking over on his

Amateur trainer Butch Goodwin casts Chesie toward water gap between two J-shaped peninsulas of land.

Chesie makes mighty water entry.

Now he's handled toward the slot.

own senses, defy your instructions and go get the duck he scents—even though it means going to shore.

So that's what we attempt to attain here. A dog that'll follow our instructions only so long as we're right, *but will overrule us and go on his own when his senses tell him we, as handlers, are wrong.* Okay?

Successfully navigating his way through the slot, he lands on far bank where dummies are seeded for fetch.

And as with all water blinds, it is imperative Chesie comes back the same way he went out, thus completing a classic field trial retrieve. But note: A general hunting dog would run down the J-shaped peninsula on the left side and leap to sea to swim to far bank.

8

The Water Blind

EVER BEEN COON HUNTING, shuffling in the soggy leaves under a full moon, the twigs and tree trunks posing eerily in the dark? Then you arrive at still water. It lies slick and fathomless and foreboding. How deep is it? you wonder. Is the bottom muck or rock? Will you be wading along and drop off into a nutria hole, and you and gun and all but your hat disappear from view, maybe never to be seen again?

Well, I've been there and I've thought those thoughts as I've faced those slashes and ponds and streams and ice-filled rivers and swamps. But the coon dogs enter water like an otter; they just slide, for they know water carries scent, carries the exact trail the coon swam along in the dark. Maybe the water's moved ten feet since the coon swam through, but the dogs puzzle it out, swim across, then backtrack ten feet to once again be on course. So you get caught up in it and go along. Or like some grizzled coon hunters once told a friend of mine out on his first hunt and confronted with a totally black drop-off into thin air, ''Just put your hands in your pockets and jump.'' He did and lived to tell the story. The hands were kept in the pockets so they wouldn't snag on anything and break a finger, hand or arm.

Well, I present all this as a way of explaining what Pup faces each time we bring him to water. Before now we had the marks to drive him forward. But now there's nothing. Just you telling Pup there's a bird out there somewhere and he's to hand his self-will over to you and enter the unknown and you'll direct him to the prize. If roles were reversed, would you do it? Really? I wonder.

SIMPLE WATER BLINDS

The law is this: *In running water blinds, you don't drill Pup to fetching anything. You drill Pup to avoid everything.* Read those two sentences again. And again. That's because every water blind poses a suction, or what's called a hazard: Something out there to trip Pup up, to veer him off course, to cause him to go to land when he should have stayed at sea, to force him to turn back or to side, be it wind or current or land or beaver dams or rocks or great stands of cover. Something is always waiting out there to defeat Pup. Plus, Pup is not in his natural element. He is at a disadvantage. And this thing—whatever it is—is using itself to some sadistic nature's benefit—all to defeat Pup. So know this before you ever start. And read those two top sentences the fourth time!

Here's where Pup's guaranteed to fail, so he requires your help. Only knowing this and honoring this can we proceed. For as I once answered a letter writer having trouble with water blinds, "Pup's like a poor dogface told to cross a mine field and enter a village. The soldier must forget about the village. It's the mine field he's got to maneuver. The soldier's real mission is not to reach the village. It's to avoid and survive the mine field—doing that he'll arrive in the village."

So we never cast Pup for the bird when running a water blind. Read that again, too. We always cast Pup away from hazards. And we never try to *wish* Pup to retrieve. Wishing will fail. We handle Pup to our objective, think Pup to it and then drive Pup to it. There ain't no other way.

THE FIRST WATER BLINDS

It stands to reason if an old, thoroughly trained, highly experienced retriever can run a water blind only by avoiding hazards, then a young, partially trained, inexperienced Pup should be trained to run water blinds without any hazards. We must build Pup's confidence before we show him the real water world. We must stay positive because everything about water blinds is negative. Therefore, all cautions we heeded in bringing Pup to water marks will hold true here—and then some! The crucial test here is to get Pup wet. Forget the poultry. A wet dog is the goal. For Pup won't necessarily want to go. Oh, you may have some miracle retriever

Pup that renders everything I say false and useless, but I'll bet you don't.

And how do we get Pup to go? We entice him, we trick him, we cajole him, we pray for him, we cross our fingers and we bite our fingernails to make him go. There is one thing that will help us and that's a splash. And the nearer the splash the more chance Pup will not only go, he'll break and go. And that's fine with me—and will be with you.

So how do we make a splash? Well, to just walk Pup to a hidden bird on water and tell him back would be what's called a "cold water blind." And, folks, that's exactly what it is. Pup's expected to start cold, to proceed cold and to finish cold. All of which is negative.

So the first blinds we present will be repeat blinds. We'll have a bird boy out there on an island or over on an off-shore or in a boat, and he'll blow the duck call to get Pup's attention, and the dummy will sail through the air to splash down like a space capsule. You send Pup for this obvious mark, and as he returns to deliver the bird to hand, the bird boy throws another bird in the exact spot the first bird landed. You take Pup's bird, wheel him about and cast him right back where he came from. Hopefully he'll take the cast and shoot off into the water. If not, have the bird boy toss a stone to splash next to the dummy. That'll trigger Pup. Then when he's returning with the dummy, have another dummy thrown. This time you take the bird from Pup and ram him for the water blind—and he goes.

Or he doesn't go. So what do you do now? Well, have the bird boy blow the duck call and pretend to throw something. Maybe this'll trigger Pup to launch. No? Well, there's one other thing you can do that is very effective, and that's sluice the water. Have the bird boy shoot a shotgun popper so the expelled wad strikes the water near the dummy and causes a cascade of spray. The gun will *boom,* the echo *varoom,* the water *splash,* and Pup will be hyped to plunge.

THE SEEDED PILE

When Pup's successfully running repeat blinds, you go to the next stage in his development. You put a bunch of dummies out there, great, stark-white dummies that float high in the water, and you get him to fetch one and then the other. If he won't go for the first one, then you'll be obliged to toss a dummy out there by the pile.

And while we're doing this, there'll be some rules we follow.

All blinds will be presented straightaway from the end of a peninsula. We'll avoid the problem of angle water entries.

All blinds will be presented out in the middle of an open pond with no breeze blowing, no current flowing, no cover to confound Pup and no decoys floating about to suck him off his intended line.

Later, after Pup is doing well on the repeat blind and the seeded blind, never again will we run him near the area of an old fall. He will remember the first fetch and want to go where he's been successful before.

By the same token, we'll never run Pup between two old falls he's just run. Which means we need a totally new peninsula and totally new running water to proceed.

And never can Pup be sent on a water blind (at this time) where some landfall poses closer to him when he picks up the retrieve than the casting line he just left. The casting line must always be the shortest way to dry dock.

And since we're using big, stark-white, fat dummies that float high on the water, Pup's running sight blinds. Later we'll switch him to scent blinds.

I recall my training as a Marine Corps rifleman. The drill instructor commanded us over the PA, "Ready, aim, fire." We learned that sequence, we leaned on that sequence. That sequence became part of the entire routine of shooting. Just as track stars lean into their starting blocks and wait for "Ready, set, go." If the "go" doesn't come in time, the guy falls forward on the cinders.

So it must be with Pup. We build a mental sequence that's all a part of the retrieve. This sequence is made of words, and in times of a pinch it'll be the words themselves that drive Pup out. When? When it's 15 degrees Fahrenheit and the snow's pelting in a thirty-knot wind and the lake is frozen ten feet out all around the edges, and Pup would rather lie in the straw in the warmth of the duck blind than enter that crazily chopped water.

That's why we mesmerize Pup with our casting hand and wait for the focus to show in Pup's eyes, and we cast Pup forcefully with the snap of the shutter—and the picture is brought to hand.

Okay, we tell Pup to heel, sit, stay, then we slide our left leg out (for a right-handed gunner) and place our casting hand next to Pup's head. We slowly rotate our hand in a tight circle, saying just above a whisper "Line, line . . . line." We keep doing this until Pup shows he's got the line, he stands, leans forward, his shoulder muscles tense (you can see them), the ears cock so the flap of them is parallel to the earth, the eyes grow bright and sharp, and you command "Back."

The "Back" is said softly if it's a routine blind. But it is barked to best the wind should the task before Pup indicate nothing but trouble and hardship. I can't emphasize enough handler body motion and tone and volume of voice. It's all we have to control Pup at our side or 200 yards to sea. That's our association.

I told you up front that all dog training was point of contact, repetition and association. Well, we're in the last of our three stages. In the stage that counts. Our voice on Pup's eardrums is all we have left. So we must know how to use our voice, to orchestrate it, to calm Pup down, to fire him up, to help him wizard out a puzzle or to drive him over a spiked beaver dam.

ADVANCED WATER BLINDS

Here's the scenario, right out of a beer commercial on Sunday afternoon football. You're surrounded by millions of dollars. Okay? But there's a catch. You have this atomic bomb strapped to your chest. But you do have a set of instructions on how to defuse the bomb. All you must do is follow point A, and B, and C and so on. But the instructions make this very explicit: You are to avoid certain circuits *and they are plainly marked.* You must keep these circuits in mind at all times, follow instructions, avoid the circuits and you'll be the richest man on earth.

And those instructions, my friends, are the same as those needed to successfully run Pup through a water blind. The goal is not to get the poultry, but to avoid the hazards. *They are plainly marked; you must keep them in mind at all times. You must proceed thoughtfully and with caution. And you can never succeed by wishing your way. In water blinds wishes never come true.*

Remember, too, there are only two hazards to really trip you up. One is a cast refusal and the other is Pup going to land instead of staying wet.

But what's this? There's an island between you and the blind retrieve. Of course there is. I told you there'd always be something out there to trip Pup up. So Pup must handle in the water. You have two options. If the island is small, handle Pup around it. If the island is large, then you must beach Pup *even though we never want him to go to land when fetching a water blind.* So it's a catch-22.

Well, it all boils down to this. Pup must hand his self-will over to you. All his excellence as a hunter and swimmer must be subordinated to you—standing 200 yards away, blowing your whistle and waving your arms. Can you see how Pup could turn you off? You sure can!

That's right, folks, there's nothing simple about this. You work out of one predicament (never go to shore), and then you're compelled to place Pup right where he should never go.

This is why it takes years to make a water-blind retriever.

So we approach it all gradually. First Pup is never given a water blind on a far shore. He never touches land. For six months he never touches land. Then the land you have him cross will always be directly before you: the island. Pup leaps, hits the water, takes four strokes and there's the land. He beaches and you whistle him down, give him a strong back and drive him to the far shore of the island. Only he balks there. So you must predict this and blow him down before he turns and pops. Now you're handling. You just saved a demerit at a hunting test. Then you really throw your upheld arm forward and give a back that would dent the armor on a bank truck. And you pray it's strong enough and Pup's honest enough to take the command and leap on to sea where the dummy is floating in open water.

But what's this? There's a peninsula sticking straight out into the water on the right-hand side. And the dummy is just beyond it. So we're going to drive Pup around the jut of land. But no! There's a thirty-mile-per-hour wind blowing straight in from the left and *Pup will never want to take an over into the wind while he's swimming.* That's right, it's a fact of life. So what do you do?

You angle Pup at the casting line and shoot him out 45-degrees into the prevailing wind hoping his drift will give him a water path that just shaves the tip of the peninsula. But now the wind blows him way to the right. So there's nothing left for you to do but beach him on the peninsula and drive him across and off the far side into the sea.

Or there's an hour-glass pinch of land (remember our two Js?). It's almost two ponds with a pinch of water between them, and you've got to drive Pup through the pinch—he can't touch shore. Yet there's a mighty wind blowing directly in from the left. So you cast Pup left and hope his drift will place him before the pinch. And should he even look at land, *you can't wish he would ignore it and make it on through.* No! You must whistle Pup down and drive him through the pinch.

Now another blind looks simple enough, you don't even notice that snag sticking up from a submerged tree trunk. Neither does Pup until he's launched. But now Pup sees it—wonders what it is—and alters course. Don't wish Pup'll change his mind and reroute. He won't. You have to change his mind for him. Hit him with the whistle and give him an over—away from the protruding snag.

Or it's the decoys he's after and you must take him off them.

Or it's a beaver dam before you, and Pup will not want to climb the

Here is one of the ultimate tests in water blinds: to beach the dog partway to the blind and then drive him off the island or point. Goodwin lines Chesie for distant water blind and dog makes cascading entry.

You can see a direct route to the blind takes him to peninsula.

Here Chesie beaches as Goodwin whistles him down. He must get the dog's attention to give him a hard back and really drive him across the peninsula and on to sea.

Dog takes back and heads for dike.

Having fetched the bird on the dike, Chesie now skims peninsula, coming back with fetch: an excellent job.

Chesie finishes out difficult water blind keeping return line.

And then delivers directly to hand.

sharp sticks. Especially since they're covered with ice. But he must. That's the direct line to the blind. So you saved all your power until he sets foot on the pile of lumber, and then you drive Pup over it with all the force at your disposal.

Now what's happened? You just had a triple water retrieve off this pond, and they've set up a test where the blind is between two of the old marks and a 100 yards further out.

Hunting test, heck. It's the real thing. Pup just picked up two downed ducks, and while he's bringing the second one in, another duck flies over, you shoot and it falls immediately between the two old marks— but 100 yards further out. That's why I told you up front: We'll train your dog to hunt and being a hunter he can place in any hunting test. Don't get your head screwed on backward. Have the dog fit to do the work and then he can play the game. Never have him geared to play the game and think he can work. It'll never happen. If you work as a cowboy, you might win a rodeo. But being a rodeo rider is not likely to make you into a ranch hand. Got it?

So now you must drive Pup between the two old falls and get him to the blind fast. Why fast? For that bird is just wing-clipped. He can revive and dive or fly away any second. We must conserve game. If Pup's hung up on old scent, or in the location of an old fall, your third bird may never get in the game bag.

I'm writing a book for hunters with hunting retrievers. As Omar Driskill says—Omar was born wearing camouflage, and for a teething ring they gave him a duck call—"I don't have no stuffed ducks hangin' in my house. I eat 'em." Omar trains his dogs to fulfill this assignment. Only naturally do they then win at hunting retriever tests.

SO WE DRILL

Therefore, to get our dogs to perform all these miracle blind retrieves—and then some—we drill and drill and drill. I'll tell you right now, running land and water blinds can become compulsive. There's been more than one divorce court see a haggard retriever (man or woman) brought to trial. "He's (she's) never home, Your Honor, and all he (she) thinks about is that damned dog!" Women are falling victim, too. Even more so now since the gals have caught the mania of handling a sure 'nuf good retriever. They used to sit at home while their husbands hunted. Now they go with them—or go alone.

So you work the dogs into the wind to learn their nose, with the wind to sharpen their sight, into a crosswind so hopefully they catch on to the fact that they should always crab downwind for a better chance of getting a snatch of scent. You work them in rain and sleet and snow and the heat of a summer day. You work them in clear water and muck and stuff that's as gunky as a skid-row diner's coffee.

You stop the car while you're out selling—oh yes, you're a traveling salesman. And yes, the dog is always with you. And you leave the dog in his crate and walk out 200 yards and plant a dummy where the dog will be obliged to run through expanses of cover and then plunge into an irrigation canal.

I was that traveling salesman once. And I'd carry the dog and gun and rubber decoys (the dekes being the kind that inflate when you drop them on the water), or I'd carry used diapers I'd buy from the diaper service to spread out for decoys on geese. Yes, I've arrived at business appointments (anyway, I did then) with mud caked to the knees of my pants and elbows of my suit coat. There are many others of equal insanity and/or dedication.

I've run land and water blinds in blizzards where ten yards away I couldn't even see the dog.

But keep it up and keep it up and keep it up, and one day you and Pup will have it. There's no alternative to hard work and repetition. And yes, there'll be many a day you'll have to show Pup that white plastic flyswatter. And other days you'll have to go to sea—even if it's ice water.

ELECTRONIC COLLARS

Now the lazy man's way of short-circuiting all this is by slapping an electric collar on Pup and casting him to sea. Every time he does wrong, sizzle him with a charge of high-voltage, low-amperage electricity. It's as easy as touching your TV remote control. And it's as disastrous for Pup as the big chair in the big house. Has his crime really fit this punishment, that he be sent to the electric chair?

Well, says my critic, I can reach Pup with that collar when there's no other way I can get to him. You mean you can't paddle a boat? You can't wade in the muck? You can't swim? Even if there's ice on the water? Then what right do you have to send a dog where you won't go? Tell me that. Do you have a reason? No, you don't. If I were Pup, I'd never work for you: You don't deserve it.

How much easier to start Pup on nightly walks where you cast him from shore and have him swim as you walk completely around the pond.

Anytime he turns to beach, you softly say, "No, Pup, keep it up." And you keep walking and singing a song for him and letting him know how happy you are. There'll come a night when Pup will sulk if he can't take this swim. I've seen Web, Mike Gould's miracle Lab, swim one mile around a pond and never look to shore when he was one year old. You think Mike has trouble controlling Web on a water blind? No! You think he has to shock him to performance? No! For he did his groundwork first, he got across his basic schooling in a pleasant way, he did it with fun and play and intimacy. What electric jolt in the neck could ever equal that?

You want an electric collar, you go ahead and buy one. But get another book to help train your dog while you're at it, for I'm not in the "fry cook" business.

TO SUM IT UP

There is no easy way to make a water blind retriever. It's all hard work. And it's all done with the knowledge that we never cast Pup for the bird, but cast him and handle him away from all hazards.

Remember what happened to the oil tanker up in Alaska? It ran aground and lost most of its liquid cargo. It ran into a disaster. The captain couldn't wish the boat around what it hit. Only could the boat be directed about it. The law at sea is always: Avoid the hazards to get to port.

It's no different for Pup.

Happy sailing.

Irrigation pipe still runs across our athletic field as Mike Gould shows us his looking-glass drill. He runs from starting point and Web is sent for distant pile of dummies.

9

The Looking Glass Drill

$\mathbf{W}$E JUST SPENT several pages where I convinced you Pup could never line a blind (get the bird without any whistles or hand signals); rather, he had to be handled to all blind retrieves by you directing him away from all hazards. That's true. A truth to hold forever.

But there's also another truth. When Pup becomes a class performer, when he does his job without error, then, and only then, can you line him for a blind. I'm talking about a dog with a built-in compass, computer and sixth sense. One that knows what hazards are, what they are meant to do to him, but his skill and knowledge is so great he takes on the hazard and overcomes it—all on his own.

Now you'll admit there was no way I could reveal this to you before. You would have been trying to *wish* Pup through the hazards, and we've proven that just won't work. But on his own Pup can wizard his way through them, and we're going to show you how to help Pup do it.

Mike Gould, our young retriever friend, the one who gave us the power bar, has also come up with a sure-fire way to get a retriever to hold his line. He calls his technique "the looking glass drill." He chose that name because, as you'll see, Pup gets the same picture going out as he sees coming in—thus guaranteeing Pup always comes back the same way he went out. An invaluable aid, for it keeps Pup from meandering around out there and stumbling upon another bird and being prompted to switch birds or try to bring in two birds at one time.

Now Mike has moved far back and Web is seen leaving the corridor of dummies and running to deliver to hand.

Here you get a broad view of the looking-glass drill (in the previous two photos the telephoto lens stacked the foreground).

HOW IT'S DONE

You heel your advanced journeyman retriever into the field and take him along as you drop a dummy, then take three more steps in a straight line and drop a second dummy. Three more steps and a third dummy is dropped. Three more steps and the fourth dummy is downed. You look back to make sure your four dummies are in a straight line.

Now you walk fifteen yards at a right angle to your row of dummies and lay out an identical column of four more dummies. The result is a corridor: two parallel rows of dummies, absolutely straight, and the rows are fifteen yards apart.

Now you heel Pup into the corridor and situate him between the first two dummies down: let's say the first two dummies in the corridor to the east. We'll call this point W. Point X would be the second row of dummies, point Y is the third row and point Z is the last row. Or said another way: The two rows of dummies correspond to the two rows of brass buttons on a military dress uniform. Point W would be the lowest row, the row nearest your belt. And point Z would be the two buttons at your neck. Okay?

Now you tell Pup to stay at point W—he's seven and a half yards from each vertical row of dummies—in the middle of the corridor, and you walk away in a straight line some twenty-five yards and lay down (or plant) three dummies. Then you return to Pup and throw a fourth dummy toward the pile to hype Pup up.

Obviously there is no suction on this drill, for it's only Pup's peripheral vision that picks up the two dummies between which he's heeled and seated. You cast him for the pile of four dummies afield and he successfully makes the fetch.

Now you move back to point X. There are two dummies angled before Pup and one dummy to each side of him.

You'll need not throw a dummy to hype Pup up, just tell him heel, sit, stay, check the angle of his back and head and cast him for the repeat blind. He'll retrieve the second dummy in the pile.

Only now you move back to point Y. There are four dummies at angle before Pup now, plus one more to each side. Cast Pup and he'll retrieve the third dummy.

Now you move back to point Z—to your last line of two dummies. Pup is confronted with six dummies at angle before him now and one to each side. You cast him for the remaining dummy afield and the simple part of the drill is completed.

Now you set the whole thing up again, only you don't stay with Pup in the corridor of dummies. Oh no. Now you move back ten yards, let's say, or twenty yards. Then you cast Pup through the corridor and he makes all his retrieves. Until finally you're 100 yards from the corridor and you drill Pup right through it as he makes his way to a pile of dummies planted 100 yards on out. So he's running a 200-yard blind. Plus, as he goes out, so he comes back. He shoots through the corridor going to the pile and he shoots through the corridor as he makes his retrieves. This makes for an honest lining dog like nothing else can.

Mike says, "The significance of it all is this: The dog learns to run an absolutely straight line off your hand cast without paying attention to any distractions, and then he turns around with the dummy in his mouth and is obliged to come back the same way."

WATER

Now let's take our looking glass drill to water. Only don't lay out the drill perpendicular to the shore. Make it an angle of at least 45 degrees. *Yes, we are finally going to have an angle water entry.* If you want, you lay out three corridors—one angling to the right, one angling to the left and the middle one heading straight into the water.

Then you stand with Pup where the three corridors meet and keep carouseling him about you until you pick the corridor you want and cast him.

Plus, and this is mighty important, as Pup goes out, so he comes in. He must beach to be in the corridor and bring the bird (or dummy) to hand. Mike tells us, "This drill is so important on water. With the looking glass drill you achieve the most critical angle water entry, plus the dog comes back at the same critical angle. You stop the dog from running the bank when he's going for a fetch and you stop the dog cheating . . . you stop the dog from looking for the nearest land to beach when he makes his retrieve to hand."

BACK TO LAND

When Pup's passed the basic tests for the looking glass drill on land and water, now we lay out our corridor—not so it's fifteen yards wide, but we make it ever narrower and narrower until finally it's only six feet wide. Now we take Pup 100 yards distant and cast him through the six-foot-wide corridor on out another 100 yards and direct him to come back the same way. Talk about an honest dog: We're really threading the needle.

But we're not finished.

All this time we've been running on level land. Now we go to hills and terrain with ditches and running water and stands of high, obstructing cover—yet Pup can still see our corridor out there—and he shoots through the eye of the storm. He holds his line no matter what the obstacles or diversions might be.

Mike says, "I did this as an experiment once for a group of dog handlers, and I actually brought the corridor down to one step . . . three feet across . . . and I was 150 yards back and the dummies were 150 yards beyond the 'pinch,' and I sent Web right through there." And adds Mike, "He wasn't two years old then."

But what do you do if Pup avoids any of these corridors, either going or coming? You verbally tell him in a loud voice, "Noooo-ooooo, nooooo-oooooo, *sit!*" Then you go out there, take Pup over to the middle of the corridor (whether he's going for the bird and is empty-mouthed or he's coming back with the bird fetched up) and tell him to sit and stay. Then you walk back to your handler's position and order Pup either to drive on for his retrieve or come in with the bird.

Mike says the reason you should shout the dog down orally instead of whistle is because he often starts his dogs on the looking glass drill before he's ever put them on whistle signals. You do as you like.

Mike further says, "I'd say the reason this drill is so good is it helps the handler generate supreme accuracy on the cast without the handler having to do it all in aiming the dog. The corridor is also aiming the dog—the corridor is forcing the dog to hold his line. This makes the obstacle the target . . . the obstacle becomes a distant gun sight."

This is magnificent dog training, for it takes something negative— the hazard—and turns it into the goal. I'll show you how that would work on a water blind. The bird is directly past the end of the peninsula. Pup must swim from shore to the peninsula—but not touch land—and then on to the waiting bird. Pup knows he's never to touch land unless ordered to do so. Thus he looks at this test from the casting line, sees the exact route down Mike's extended hand *and knows he must shave the point.* In other words, what has been the hazard before, now becomes the aid. And all because of the looking glass drill.

"But," Mike warns us, "when the dog starts looking for the corridor, and all of them will, then I phase it out and never use it again. And this takes only a few weeks. But I'll tell you this, it's really an uplifting device for dogs that have a confidence problem. You know the dog that sits at heel and starts looking all around, or cringing down, and he's telling you he would rather be somewhere else. After this drill they sit down and just go 'bing.' They're aimed. They're eager. And they want to run.''

WRAPPING UP

To make certain Pup's taking direct casts off your hand, place him at the right-hand side of the corridor and run him through at an angle so he emerges just shaving the first dummy dropped on the left. Then reverse it. Then step back and run it. Then go 20 yards, 50 yards, 100 yards back. For this is really what we're teaching Pup: He is to follow the exact direction of the cast of your hand. He is aimed as surely as you aim a rifle. And he is to go as straight as the fired bullet.

But in closing there's one major hazard on water we've still to discuss, and that's decoys. And the rule to remember here is this: Whatever is to be taught on water must first be shown on land. So that's where the decoys are scattered, and you help Pup through them. Let him sniff them. Then you stand on one side of the spread and throw a dummy over the pile. Send Pup through the decoys to get the fetch. When he has it all down pat, then you go to water. You should have no trouble.

Do the same with working out of a boat (we discussed this before). The boat should always be dragged up on land. Have Pup cast out of it, jump in and out of it, have him sit in it while you stand and rock the thing back and forth. Let him get assured about the boat, and let him get comfortable in the boat, then, and only then, do you take the boat and Pup to sea.

One last thought on running blinds is this. At a hunting test you'll be given a dry popper. Now a popper is a shotgun shell with no shot. And the person who fires this shell is also called a popper. You heel Pup up to a casting line and he sees nothing. No bird flies, nothing happens, when all of a sudden off to side, or way to field, someone is seen (or not seen) who fires a popper, maybe once or twice.

This is to simulate a gunner having killed a bird outside Pup's field of vision. The test is to cast Pup—not get a cast refusal—have him go to field or go to sea and hand his self-will entirely over to you. But there is something else that occurs. What if the popper is standing ten feet from you, and Pup gets hung up on the sound of the gun and the guy standing there and he wants to cast that way? Well, this is another time we've had to tell Pup no on the casting line. It is negative, and it is confusing for Pup.

Professional hunting retriever trainer Jeff Devazier entices a ten-week-old Chesie pup into boat by dancing minidummy and blowing whistle.

Now the pup exits boat to get scurrying dummy...

... and runs forward to leap for dummy just before Jeff throws it to water.

But tell him no you do, and carousel him about you and set him up to be aimed toward the blind. But he may refuse you and keep looking at the popper. Never mind. Just point your hand at the man, tell Pup no and carousel him about you once again. Keep doing this until you erase the popper from Pup's mind. You know when he's zeroed in—you know how to read him—so that's when you cast.

Something else that comes up in this: Pup will come to the line and see three sets of guns in the field. They'll sound off in retort and a thrown bird: one, two, three. Only as Pup is bringing in the third bird down, the first two sets of gunners and bird boys will retire (that is, they'll hide). So when Pup hands you the bird and turns around, he'll only see one set of guns standing out there. Which means he will really need to mark the birds down, not think he can cast off the guns.

Well, we've been through this before. If you see Pup refuse to mark, that is, he turns his head even before the bird hits the water or ground, then send him for that fetch. You'll soon have him waiting the whole flight of the bird out.

For once he's learned to mark the bird and not the gun, it matters not if the gunners retire or stay.

And what of the pop on water? That's where Pup's heading for a mark or blind but suddenly turns about for you to help him. When you see him start to turn, hit him with the whistle. Then when he's looking at you, give your arm signal. You can do this both in training and in a test hunt. You want to appear to the judges as having whistled the dog down—instead of him popping. In training, however, you don't do this. When you see the dog popping and don't get on the whistle fast enough to look like you controlled him, then you flat turn your back on Pup. You peek back, and when he finally moves, then you hit him with the whistle. He must learn he only stops or turns when you command him to do so.

In training an advanced retriever, there's something else you do to help Pup. At a test hunt the gunners, the boys who throw the birds and the boys who plant the blinds are supposed to be motionless and silent. Alas, that's not always the case. Consequently, they distract Pup. So have your own help talk and move about when Pup's working in practice. It will prepare him to ignore these people during the running of the test hunt—or while out hunting where there are usually people moving and talking.

That's about it. Only I'd like to close out blinds and marks by saying again: You can't wish Pup to a bird, you've got to drive him there. And the only way he can be successful is by avoiding (or handling) all hazards. Sure, you can line the blind—get there with no whistle or hand signals—it's spectacular, everyone wants to do it. But in the long run it's the cautious handler and the honest dog that wins in the field or at a test hunt.

And remember, run some blinds with a gun in your hand. You'll have to do it while hunting and during the running of some test hunts. And remember, too, have the safety on that gun and the breach open.

10

Pup and the Gun

ANYONE WHO'S TRAINED one gun dog can tell you how to introduce a retriever to the gun. The system's simple because Pup loves to eat. You put down Pup's food bowl and walk off 100 yards and fire a .22 blank cartridge in your training pistol, and if Pup stops eating, or worse, yet, runs away, then you've got trouble.

But this is hardly likely. I doubt if Pup even looks up. He'll keep on chomping, so the next night you only go eighty yards, then sixty, forty, twenty, ten—and finally you stand right at the food bowl and empty the revolver, and Pup looks up to say, "You got any more of this, coach . . . this is good stuff." It even gets to where you can walk out of the house, lay down the food pan, fire the pistol and Pup will run to eat.

So that's one way of introducing the gun, but there's another method I prefer. All the while you're Happy Timing and Pup's out 100 yards— hopefully running with other dogs—you fire the blank training pistol. Pup'll likely stop and look back at you, but you're looking the other way, or you're reaching up to a tree limb. That is, you don't acknowledge in any way a shot was fired—or heard.

Then you walk on and fire again. Not excessively, just every now and then, especially when Pup's very involved, like chasing a butterfly.

The reason I prefer introducing the gun while Happy Timing is that the report is heard afield where it will always naturally be. In Pup's mind it will become a part of the grass and hills and shrubs and sky and water.

It will be a natural part of nature and in nature is where you and Pup will work and live.

But what if Pup proves to be gun-shy?

THE GUN-SHY DOG

Well, let's get our terms right before we proceed. Looking at the whole spectrum of gun dogdom—mongrels through those bred in the purple—you will see a range in disposition that runs from terrified under the gun to dauntless. Now a gun-shy dog will cringe under the gun or even run away. But this you must know: A true gun-shy dog is terrified of everything. He cowers before man, noise, weed cover, birds, taking a ride in the family car, a guest entering the house or even the ringlets caused by lapping in a water bowl. God just wound these dogs' motors too tight; you shuffle a foot and they'll jump. I feel so sorry for them; their stomachs must be running hot with acid.

Such is the classic gun-shy dog, and there is no cure.

Now there are extrasensitive dogs that may cringe before the gun until they become accustomed to it. And there are other dogs that because of accidents or misjudgments in the field on the part of the handler temporarily don't want to be around a gun. *But these are not gun-shy dogs.*

Let me give you an example: Pup's in the duck blind, the gunner rises to fire, a twig catches his coat sleeve and slaps Pup's face just as the gun goes off. Now Pup is man-shy, gun-shy, bird-shy (he saw the flying duck) and cover-shy. All accomplished in one second. But is this Pup truly gun-shy? No! A training error has occurred and must be corrected. Pup got hit in the face (we can handle this); he didn't get wired wrong in the womb (we can't fix that).

And how do we correct the accident-caused gun-shy dog? *We do it with other dogs.* No better way. What we must do is bold up the errant pooch. There are many ways to do this: The magic table, for example, will help get the job done. For shy dogs grow strong in disposition when worked there.

And tons of birds—they'll eventually cure Pup. *For you must know there is no gun-dog problem that can't be cured with birds.* The reason is that birds are in Pup's breeding, in the blood, indelible. For thousands of years his forebears hunted and fetched birds. Pup's got that in his blood: There's bird craziness in there somewhere. And with tons of birds we can bring it out. Pup will forgive the report of the gun because of his love of birds. But I'm talking expense now: I'm talking about shooting hundreds of birds.

But to get Pup over gun-shyness fast, with the least fuss, the greatest success and the happiest dog, you do it with other dogs.

Remember our chain gang? Well, snap a string of dogs there (including Pup) and release each dog, one by one, to work birds. But don't release Pup. When that bird flies before that string of dogs and that gun goes off and the working dog is sent for the fetch, you'd better have a stout chain system, for it's going to be tested. The dogs on there will flip, leap, try to bite the dog next to them (thus the sixty-six-inch spacing in drop chains), dig holes, spin about, bark and generally go berserk. We make Pup agonize as we train his kennel mates. But, alas, what amateur trainer has all these prospective gun dogs?

Well there's a way: what I call the walking chain gang.

THE WALKING CHAIN GANG

Obtain the services of an all-age gun dog, one staunch on wing and shot, a sure performer. Let him be extrasteady, reposed, completely sure of himself. And where do you come by such a dog? You either ask a pro to work with you (and some will), or you team up with a buddy and work each others' dogs, or you join a hunting retriever club.

Now take your gun-shy Pup and couple him with another dog: ideally one a little advanced in holding steady to shot and wing. And when I say couple, that's exactly what I mean. Have two dogs on one split-end rope. One end going to one dog's collar, the other end going to the gun-shy dog's collar. (And, yes, there's a ready-made device you can buy for this from any gun dog supply house.) Now these two dogs are walked in tandem by a helper, while in front another handler works the all-age dog.

Plant some birds, lots of birds, in the tufts of grass you've left unmowed in a bird field, or have your birds planted in brush piles or natural clumps of thicket. Whatever. Just have birds planted along your course either in release traps or retained in holding pens where a bird boy can take them to hand and loft them to the wind.

Work the all-age dog into the scent cone of each bird, tell him to heel, sit, stay, then you go forward and kick out the bird—but don't fire. Never fire. Let the trio of dogs watch the launched bird fly off. Now go on to the next planted bird. This time you can stay next to the all-age dog and release the trapped bird via remote control. Or you can stay with the

Two dogs can be hooked in tandem with a Y connector.

Gun-shy dog and advanced dog follow all-age retriever. Bird boy throws dummy and makes "pow" sound with his voice. Later he'll actually carry and fire a gun. All dogs mark dummy down.

The two dogs in reserve must agonize as working dog gets to fetch dummy. This puts a fire in the tandem team, to be sure. And that's how you bring a dog out of gun-shyness.

dog and have a bird boy walk forward and release a bird from the holding pen. Work any of these combinations and work them over and over. As you do so, keep an eye on the gun-shy dog. He'll tell you what progress he's making.

Remember, you can't train a dog unless you can read him. Don't be illiterate. Learn Pup's language. Pup is constantly sending you messages. Learn them, abide by them, honor them. In the beginning, for example, the gun-shy dog will either be hangdog or zany. He'll either drag along or go bonkers. Just have the helper keep a tight rope on the tandem and move on. Incidentally, that other dog in tandem is broken to wing and shot, so he's placid, and Pup senses this: That placidity rubs off. That's why that dog is there. He's the confidence builder. As is the all-age dog up front.

Later you'll begin to see the gun-shy dog settling. He'll be watching the working dog, plus he'll be sensing and responding to the dog to which he is coupled. *What's more, he'll become entranced with the flying bird.*

After you've gone afield several days with no gun, go several more.

Now you put the gun-shy dog in the lead and hook the all-age dog and the brace dog in tandem. They now follow with the helper. Work the gun-shy dog into the bird's scent cone, and have the bird launched one way or the other. *Only, here you cast the gun-shy dog to chase the bird.* Do this several days. Finally the gun-shy dog will break (hurrah!), and you let him go, let him have fun, let him run to the skyline if he wants. And why the two dogs following in tandem? For days Pup's been afield with these two dogs and nothing bad has happened to him. He's developed confidence in them and you and the helper and the field. Now let's get him crazy about birds. Incidentally, if we're using pigeons most of them will be flying back to your home coop, so you're not out a dime in birds.

When all's going well—and once again the gun-shy pup will tell you exactly where he is in training—you will now take a gun to field. *When the dog is chasing the released bird and is distant, fire the shotgun one time.* If the dog does not stop, turn around or in any way acknowledge the gun, you have just scored a training success.

Do this many more days. Always, dog training takes at least twice as long as you feel it does, or it should. But it does, and that's the law of the game—the unbreakable law.

Anytime you have to correct a problem, you usually create another problem. For now we have a dog that's not gun-shy, but he breaks on game. So it's back to yard training and heel, sit, stay. And then you gradually work him into single dummy marks, then finally marks with a training pistol and the gun and so on.

Distancing Pup from the gun in early training encourages here the first introduction to marking off the gun. Girl throws bird, distant gunner to the right-oblique fires, handler holds dog (but not gun), starting Pup honors from the far back. Gradually gun is moved nearer until handler does the firing and extra gunner is no longer needed.

Now let's back up.

All this was accomplished with the walking chain gang. Unfortunately the procedure requires the aid of a helper. And once again, that's where the pro has the advantage. If successful, he has someone on the payroll. But you? You've got to beg and borrow. Best you join a gun dog club with others of like mind (and like need) and help each other. There can be no other way. Unless you talk a pro into letting you train with him. And your payback for that is to help him around the kennels or serve as his bird boy.

And while we're backed up, let's study a phenomenon. I've said it before and will again. I do not know how dogs communicate. It is extrasubtle. I'll give you an example. My African safari friends have told me a pack of African hunting dogs (maybe twenty) will be lying on an open grass field, essentially all asleep, when suddenly all twenty heads will come up at the same time. Who sensed what (not all twenty, that would be incredible) and how was it communicated to the pack? How do you, at home, explain your dogs triggering to a strange dog going down the street with the house locked up, the TV blaring, the odors of supper hanging in the air? Yet the dogs trigger as one and bombard the door getting out to challenge this interloper. What has been the channel(s) of communications, what was the message, what were the sensors?

I don't know. All I know is it exists. So the gun-shy dog on the walking chain gang is in constant communication with the all-age dog up front, the partially broke dog hooked in tandem, the helper, you, the cover, the sky, the wind, the bird, everything. We make the mistake of seeing it all as ultrasimple. Ha! It is so complex and intriguing I'll go to my grave baffled and frustrated that I could never break it all down, I could never understand it.

Just use it. That's all you have to do. Just recognize there are hundreds of forces going on between the three dogs and you and your helper as you cross the bird field—and pay attention. If something happens to confuse you, sit down and think it out. Maybe you'll need to change dogs. But never, never go blindly forward and think you'll luck out. You won't.

Constantly read what each dog is telling you and honor what you think you decode. Only when you do this are you a dog trainer. And it's only a dog trainer who can cure a gun-shy dog.

11

A Bird in Hand

THIS IS THE MOST important chapter in this book, but because I know you I can predict you won't think so. That's because a magazine columnist always gets mail from readers when an article interests them, and from 1985 through 1990 I ran an intensive educational campaign in *Field & Stream* about the importance of birds in gun dog training and hardly got a postcard. The ten and a half million readers said, "That's for the birds."

Gun dog trainers think a dummy can suffice, that it can be an effective substitute for a bird, and it just ain't so. Your retriever is a bird dog: *Bird is half the name, the first half, the important half.* It is as impossible to train a bird dog without a bird as it is to teach marksmanship without a gun.

THE PIGEON

God's gift to the retriever trainer was the common barnyard pigeon. These can be purchased as culls from an established pigeon fancier or trapped in church belfries, under bridges or out of flour mills. But don't buy homers. Should they escape, they'll simply go home. But the offspring of homers that are born on your place will home to your own coop. They can be invaluable in birdying up a gun-shy pup, remember?

We catch pigeons with a trap consisting of a box outfitted with

These hanging bobs are stationary in a pigeon coop. They may also be installed in a portable trap you take to field.

Here is a typical portable trap. Bait with grain and leave bobs tied up for three days, then drop bobs and pigeons will push them open to enter and be unable to exit.

This is a major coop capable of handling many birds. Entrance through bobs is to the left, then pigeons turn right to enter enclosed area.

swinging bobs at one end and a gate in the top you can reach through and retrieve the bird. Bobs are rigid metal wires looped over an axle and hanging, free-swinging, like a curtain of harem beads. Bobs are hung on the inside of the box and a half-inch longer than the door's threshold. Therefore, birds can push the bobs up to enter, but the bobs then catch against the threshold, and when the bird tries to exit, he's trapped.

You get the maximum harvest out of a trap by baiting it with grain, tying up the bobs and letting the pigeons get a free lunch for three days. Once accustomed to entering the box for food, the pigeons will then push up the dropped bobs to enter—and you've got 'em.

Take your pigeons home to a coop. Most anything will do. I've seen some of the most awful looking shambles serve as a pigeon condo, and I've seen some Taj Mahals. What's needed is a screened-in area where the birds can fly about (say eight feet wide, eight feet deep and six feet tall). You have a doorway where you enter to bring food and water and a little sand and to clean the place up (the sand is for the gizzard to help grind the cracked corn).

Each pigeon has his own compartment made of plywood. There they will raise their young, and you'll have more pigeons in a year than you ever thought possible. If you live in cold country, have a wind barrier to the north, but realize the pigeon is hearty. He can take both the heat and the cold. Yet in the summer I always put a tarp over my setup to keep the noon sun from baking down.

Homing pigeons must have a way to enter but no way to exit. So once again the coop is outfitted with a set of bobs and a balcony on the inside where the pigeon can enter and stand, then fly to his compartment.

Your primary loss in a pigeon coop will come from predators. A mink can wipe you out in one night. So the place must be built secure. Mighty secure.

Now when you're ready to work your pigeons, you enter with a large fishing net, catch what you need and put these birds in a tote box made of wood on all six sides that has two overlapped sections of inner tube in the top where you can knife your hand down and take a bird to hand. When you're working in the field, place the box out of the sun.

HANDLING THE PIGEONS

There are several ways to hobble a pigeon so it can still fly but not be able to escape. The favorite practice across America is to pull out a particular number of primary flight feathers in one wing. You pull these feath-

Legs are immobilized by wrapping them just above the knee joint.

Pigeon flight feathers are those to the right of the man's thumb. Pull as many as you want for controlled flight.

Bird is grasped in hand correctly when fingers encompass bone and gristle in forefront of both wings.

An excellent homemade tote for taking pigeons to field is a plastic bucket with two strips of overlapping inner tube installed in the lid.

ers from the body out toward the wing tip. Pull all but four flight feathers and the bird will fly about 100 yards. Pull all but three flight feathers and the bird will fly seventy-five yards. Pull all but two flight feathers and the bird will fly from twenty-five to thirty yards before it goes down. This seemingly does not hurt the bird: I've had pigeons die of old age in my coop. But the wings have been immobilized enough to give a good flight for Pup to see but not sufficient for the pigeons to "fly the coop," as they say.

If the pigeon is to be fetched by the dog—and not fly away as an enticement—then wrap a new pipe cleaner about the pigeon's legs (just above the knee) so when he lands he can't walk away. Keep using new cleaners and you'll never cut into the flesh.

You'll have pigeons of different colors. Use great, fat, stark-white birds for starting Pup, and when you're finishing him out, you can pick the dun-colored birds. This will make Pup use his nose.

Now there's a way to throw a pigeon (or any bird). Take both wings in one hand with the neck and head toward the front. You'll feel a frontal bone and gristle in each wing and you grasp this mass to effect a hearty toss. Then you throw the bird underhanded and he beats his wings for loft. Don't throw pigeons in water: How'd you like your arms impeded and your legs tied and be tossed to sea?

Once again, the bird boy must practice throwing the bird. It's simple once you get the hang of it, but in the beginning the pigeon can be thrown to ground, over the bird boy's head or who knows where.

SUZIE

The second mainstay of the retriever trainer is the pen-raised mallard, called a Suzie. These birds are worked on water and can be hobbled in many ways. Once again I tie the legs with a new pipe cleaner, just above the knee, so the bird can't swim away. The wings are impeded by wrapping a pipe cleaner about the base of both wings and tying them above the back. In the old days we used rags. And for a beginning Pup retrieving ducks on water we'd cut a four-inch inner tube section to slip over the bird's body and hold the wings tight so there'd be no splashing. That further meant Pup had to fetch the bird, instead of dragging it in by one wing tip.

Omar Driskill ties ducks with duct tape: taping one wing to the body and both legs together. As I say there are many ways to immobilize a bird. Use what suits you.

Trainers hobble mallard's leg with surveyor tape.

One wing can be taped to the body so pup will have a better chance of grasping bird.

This duck is hobbled with surveyor tape about legs and base of wings.

But never, never, never throw one of these ducks on land. They cannot break their fall and will hit to likely hemorrhage. We must be as kind to our birds as we are to our dogs. We don't want them distressed or hurt. And when Pup's brought you a bunch of ducks, always lay them out separately on the grass so they can dry, never pile them in a clump.

To house ducks you need a chain-link pen on lots of sand to be used to grind corn in the gizzard. Put a tub of water in there (or have a stream flow through) for them to splash about in and a roof over one section so they can get in out of bad weather and intense sun. Again, you must worry about, and prepare for, predators.

You can transport ducks to field in an orange crate and tie them up on location. Again you rig a self-closing set of two rubber inner tube strips through which you reach to secure a bird. And yes, carriers are ready-made to be bought at the gun dog supply store.

OTHER GAME BIRDS

There's not a bird you can't train Pup with: chukar, pheasant, Hungarian partridge, prairie chicken, bobwhite, blue grouse and even guinea fowl (which, incidentally, were imported into this country for the sole and express purpose of gun dog training). But I don't want you to try raising any of these birds. When you have a need, buy them from an established game bird breeder. That is, those birds that can be raised in captivity. With the species that can't be domesticated, you naturally work them in the wild.

Remember how I taught you it was impossible to wish Pup to a blind retrieve? Well, it's equally impossible to train Pup on dummies and expect him to perform opening day on wild game afield. Here's what will happen.

DOLLY PARTIN

It was probably the first American Kennel Club hunting retriever test hunt held in western America, and Mike Gould and I were judges. We started that day with puppies, and up to the line came a thickset, heavy-duty, easy-moving young man with a roly-poly yellow Lab pup about nine months old. We explained the test to the handler. We were going to toss a single, shackled duck into a small pond while the guns fired and the pup was to run through the mixed cover, glop in the mud, fetch up the duck and return it to the line.

The lad's manner indicated "Nothin' to it."

The guns fired, the duck arced from the bird boy's hand, splatted in the pond, and the handler flashed a hand up, ordering "Back" as the frisky pup launched from the casting line, smashed the brittle cover and leaped to the gumbo. Then, big-footed, she glopped toward the duck and jutted out her chin to fetch it up just when the duck raised her head to clear her throat and gave a resounding *quack*. Whereupon the pup leaped straight up in the air, came down going partially the other way and raced back to the line with the whites of her eyes glancing back at the vocal duck.

The handler was crushed, the gallery hilarious, the judges quizzical and the dog devastated.

Now I sensed many things. This was a good kid, I could tell it in his manner and in his eyes. He had a swell pup. This had to be the first test hunt for either of them. If things were left the way they'd come unraveled, it could well be their last. I took stock. Then I picked up a dead duck, handed it to the lad and told him, "Take this duck back to that dirt road and give it to your pup. Make that pup carry it at heel up and down that road . . . let her rest . . . then make her carry it some more. Being real gentle about all of it, okay? And it's hot . . . give her plenty of water."

When the first puppy test was finished, I went back to the road to find the lad and asked him, "How's she doin'?"

"Great," he told me.

So I granted another concession. You see, you can't train on test hunt grounds and that's what I instructed the lad to do. Also, in the old field trial format you couldn't run a dog out of contention. If a dog failed a test he was out for the day. Now I offered to carry the dog the rest of the day out of contention—which you can do at a test hunt so the handler and dog get practice—and this way the boy could turn the test hunt into a training session. Remember: I told you judges should be called helpers and how the game would change!

Nobody objected to letting the lad run "free," but I would have been unmovable if they had. It's not important to me to be popular, only to be right. That's why most of my life I've been a majority of one. Only part of the purpose of a test hunt is to make up champions. The other and more important part, to my way of thinking, is to get an owner and his or her dog together on the right path so they both become skilled and joyful hunters.

When lunchtime came, I searched the lad out and found he and his young family eating sandwiches in a trailer. I asked to enter, sat and shared their hospitality. Then I inquired, "How could you enter a pup in a stake like this and never have her on birds?"

Jim Partin of Avondale, Colorado—that was the lad's name and home—confided, "I never expected to win. I just came to see what I needed to learn. I've been training her, mister. Yes sir, I have. I read the books and they talked about putting the pup on hand signals and that's what we've been doing."

"Hand signals," I groaned.

"Yeah . . . anything wrong with that?"

"Wrong! Better said, could there be anything right about it?" Then I asked, "What do you do to make a living, Partin?"

"I'm a fire medic."

"And," I asked, "I assume when you were three years old, your folks had you invading burning houses and rescuing children, is that right?"

"Of course not."

"Then why in the name of all that makes sense would you not allow this pup to have a puppyhood? Your folks apparently let you have a childhood, right? They let you learn your trade when you were mature enough to grasp it. Right?"

I'll always remember to Partin's credit he didn't sulk at my scolding. Instead, he brightened and said right out, "Yes sir. That's exactly the way it was."

"So . . ." I charged.

"So," he answered, "that's the way it'll be. What do you want me to do?"

"Have fun. Run in the fields with your pup. Swim in the creek with her. Tease her with barnyard pigeons you trap . . . lot's of 'em. Make her birdy . . . crazy birdy . . . and most of all, make her crazy loving about you."

Five years later and the Hunting Retriever Club calls to invite my attendance at their Grand Hunt at Mount Blanca, Colorado. They are going to honor me as the godfather of the hunting retriever movement and Omar Driskill as its founder. Incidentally, Mount Blanca is only twenty miles east down the road from Alamosa, where Dolly met the quacking duck. This is a Champion of Champions event I am told. There'll be some thirty hunting retriever champions run from all over the nation, and the best will be named Grand Champions.

My wife and I agreed that cabin fever lay upon us, so we loaded the wagon and headed for Mount Blanca.

As we pull up to the lodge bedecked with banners heralding this event, and before I can even get the engine shut off, a great hulk of a man blackens my car window. I ease the door open to have a catcher's mitt–sized hand thrust forward, grabbing my own hand and shaking my arm until I fear for shoulder separation.

"It's me . . ." the man cheers, "Jim Partin, remember?"

I do. I search for words. I ask, "And what are you doing here, Jim?"

"I'm running in the Grand Hunt, that's what. Dolly's qualified. Yes sir."

"You mean," I falter, "Dolly who jumped when the duck quacked?"

"The one and only," beams Partin.

"You've made her a hunting retriever champion?" I ask.

"You and me," corrects Partin. "We made her a hunting retriever champion."

"We?" I mumble. "I haven't seen you in five years."

"Don't matter. You put me on the way. I know it and Dolly knows it."

I stand there without knowing what to say.

Jim tells me, "I did what you told me, and Dolly just trained herself. Why she was a champion by the time she was two years old."

The next day breaks hot and windless. I find Jim Partin as tormented as a man who's slept the night in a goat shed. He worries about this and that. Then the birds are thrown, the guns go off and the test hunt is underway. Dolly does her stuff. You know her real name is Dolly Partin. A deep-chested, good-looking blonde, built like a missile silo. Only this Dolly Partin can't sing. She just fetches bird . . . after bird . . . after bird.

When it's all over, Dolly is a Grand Champion. The only guy happier than me is Jim Partin. The guy who had a pup that leaped from a quacking duck and took her all the way to test-hunt glory. And he did it with tons of love, birds and drills. The same as you can do.

So don't skimp on birds. Trap them, house them and use them. The result will be a bird dog: Anything else would just be a dog.

WILD BIRDS

Remember, too, you can hunt wild birds in off-season (where game regulations make sense), only not to shoot to kill but just to work your pup. Bird dog pros do it every summer on the North Dakota and Canadian

This Lab has flushed a wild cock pheasant while training.

prairies, questing for Huns and prairie chicken. And recall Mike Gould training Web on blue grouse at 10,000 feet in Colorado. To really make a retriever birdy, hunt him all summer on bobwhite. Nothing else has that skitter and scamper and that slapping wing beat to really put bird craziness into a dog.

But in actual hunting, beware of a few game bird species. Make sure during hunting season you shoot your cock pheasants dead before casting a young pup for a retrieve. Cock pheasants have spurs and beaks designed to do damage. And a big goose can wing-beat a pup nearly to death. Just use common sense. You don't send a Honda to tow a Kenworth truck.

TO FIELD AND STREAM

Well, you and Pup have worked hard for this moment—not that you haven't had fun doing so, for you have—and now it's time to hit the fields and streams and marshes. It's time to go bird hunting. This is what it was all done for, all dreamed about, all planned around. I hope you and Pup have the happiest of all times afield in golden grass and water shimmering under God's sunlight. I wish you birds and love and togetherness. I wish you happiness.

Let's get going.

This hunting retriever test simulates a dove hunt. Handler has gun and sits on stool, dog at heel. Judge signals bird boy hidden behind tree to launch bird. In actual hunt man and dog would be hidden and a grain field or pond would lie before them.

12

Early Bird Hunts

DOVE AND TEAL are the first bird hunts of the season for most of us. These sizzlers peel down from the north like sabre jets and buzz our water and land blinds with both Pup and you in a sweat. Pup drooling, you soaking in a short-sleeve shirt, as Pup gains respite from a block of ice you've lugged to field and you drink quarts of ice-cold Tang.

The test here is how to handle a hot dog. Or rather, how to keep an otherwise hot dog cool in hot weather. For the one secret to top gun dog performance in hot weather is *never let the dog get hot in the first place.* I've likened it many times to a car's radiator. Keep it filled with water and it'll run all day in the desert, but let it once go dry and overheat and you'll be sitting by the side of the trail until the coyotes howl and the moon lunges by.

It all starts at home. You get Pup loaded without too much excitement, and that's hard to do: You've got a crazy, birdy dog there and he's seen the gun, and even if this is his first bona fide outing, he seems to have a premonition of what awaits him. Drive him to the bird field with all the windows down for good cross ventilation, or with the air conditioning on should you have such a luxury, or a block of ice in Pup's crate if you don't.

When you arrive at the bird field, walk slowly to your bird stand (we're going after dove). Don't let Pup run ahead, don't let him get excited or hot. When you get to the tree by the pond you've scouted, ease

Pup down in the shade, put the block of ice beside him and let him lie in the puddle of thawed water. Even soak a gunny sack in cold water and lay it over Pup, let the breeze blow through it. Or simply pour water over Pup and let the wind blow-dry him.

Then when the birds come in, keep Pup settled, don't let him jump up. Make him heel, sit, stay . . . even charge. Yes, charge. That's another command for us. It comes from Great Britain and it means the dog lies flat to ground. You teach charge by attaching a cord to Pup's leather collar, then thread the cord under your boot between heel and sole, then as you command "Charge," you pull the cord to force Pup's neck to earth as you lean over and press his rump down. Not only is charge necessary to keep a cool dog at a dove blind, but it is also imperative to keep a dog lying still as you paddle across ice-filled water in a winter duck hunt. Should Pup stand he'll probably capsize the boat. Make him lie flat. And you keep reading him, knowing those shoulder muscles have to twitch before the leg can move.

Now the next thing you do is give Pup a drink of water. There's a way to do this. Have Pup sit, you reach over and pull out the side flap of his bottom lip, there'll be a pouch formed between lip and jaw, and you pour water into this pouch. Pup laps by throwing his tongue under (not over), and the water that puddles in his lower mouth will be flipped down his throat.

Five minutes after the first watering, water again. Then ten minutes later, water him again. And so on: all on the above-stated principle that if we keep Pup cool he'll stay cool. But let him once get hot, and there wouldn't be enough water in the Mississippi to cool him down. For once heated, Pup'll start to pant, which will bring slobber, and the slobber will turn to suds, and Pup will not retrieve. And I mean sticky suds: You can pick it up from the earth like Silly Putty.

And it's this Silly Putty that will force Pup to quit you. That's right, he'll cast to get the dove and stand there looking back, telling you, "If you want this feather pillow, you can come get it yourself." For the feathers are soft and cling easily to the suds of Pup's mouth and he fusses with them, dragging his jaw in the dirt or grass, trying to disengage the feathers with his big feet, trying to spit, but gagging instead. So you keep Pup's mouth water-slick with frequent watering and he can retrieve the soft-feathered dove all day. And when Pup does bring the bird in, take it from Pup immediately and then groom Pup's mouth, using your hand to wipe down the lips and remove the sticky feathers. Don't let Pup fuss with them or he'll get hotter yet.

Another hunting retriever test duplicates early teal hunt with both men in a hide with dog to side and each hunter blowing duck calls. In actual hunt the hide would be directly before the men and dog.

EARLY TEAL

Now we've placed Pup in our stamped-down tule duck blind to await the tipsy-turvy flight of the blue-winged (they're usually first) teal. They come with early pintail, so know your duck identification before you fire.

Pup's now working in water, which makes his day more enjoyable than a dusty dove field. But nevertheless, this may be tepid water. Pup thinks he can slake his thirst by drinking it, but he just gets hotter. Yet, having gotten wet by retrieving a duck or two, Pup is now wet and the air will cool him as it blows through the coat.

All cautions apply to early-season duck hunting as they do to dove. Only thing different here is Pup exerts more energy swimming than he does running on dry land. So monitor him closely. You'll think he couldn't be hot standing in water, swimming in water, but he can be.

If Pup starts to dry out, then cast him to water just to get wet so the air can cool him.

Incidentally, as with dove, the teal are laid apart from Pup so he doesn't piddle with them between kills. Pup'll do it. He'll get bored and wander over there and pick one up to bring to you. He's impatient and he wants action. But you know better. He's getting all the action he needs in this hot weather, and Pup's staying cool must be foremost in your mind.

Should Pup gag on feathers or debris scooped up when he made his retrieve on either dove or teal, then lay him flat on his side, place your hands on top of each other over the lower rib cage and exert down with thoughtful force, i.e., you're giving artificial respiration. If this thing just won't blow free, then pick Pup up by his hind legs, hanging him head down, and give him a sharp slap either high across the back of his shoulders or across the front of his chest.

If a small object's lodged in the throat, it may jar out, or you may stimulate coughing, which can blow it free. Remember, never stick your fingers down Pup's throat. He may reflex bite and/or you might lodge the object even deeper.

The celebrated vet, Dr. Dick Royse of Wichita, Kansas (you'll meet him later), recently had a hot-weather-hunt retriever brought into his clinic. The dog had actually swallowed a dove and it was stuck in his throat. Doc was able to push the dove on into the dog's stomach with a probe and the dog's life was saved. So things can turn serious on a hunt; be watchful for the unsuspected.

Besides, these early season hunts are break-in periods for the big event when the weather turns cool and the big game heads south. To that goal we'll now turn our guns.

13

China Bird

$\mathbf{T}$HE PHEASANT is the only bird I've ever known that when hunted will in turn hunt you. Not to meet you, but to avoid you. To gauge your path, and time your movement, and assess your skill, then use this thimble of knowledge to cackle at yet another dawn.

Most game birds will trust to their plumage to be one with the earth and then hesitate too long before a dog's nose. Others will drift to the call, and some to the decoy, and others to the bait. But not the China bird. He is born of the same blood as fighting cocks and he doesn't come to hand without a fight. He is in feather what the elephant and the lion and the African buffalo are in hide. He knows man and hates him and will double-back on him—not to kill him as animals will, but to at least outwit him and leave him standing with poised gun and wilted pride.

Except for the turkey, sage grouse, sandhill crane and some geese, he's our largest game bird. Yet that's misleading, since twenty-two to twenty-three inches of his total thirty-six-inch length can be in tail feathers. A cock can weigh four or five pounds and he's mostly meat. His breast dries when oven-roasted, but stew him in a pot and you've got something.

Pheasants are not found everywhere in the United States. They are a predominantly farm-belt bird, though their first successful import was to Corvallis, Oregon.

The pheasant is a very strange bird. He's beautiful enough to denote

Yellow Lab bumps cock pheasant from cover: Hunter has a good chance of downing this bird.

elegance. I've seen him mounted and strutting, in taxidermy, down the table as a centerpiece in a French estate when dining with my betters after hunting pheasant outside Orleans. But this same bird is akin to a carnival fighter. If a human, he'd have hair on his shoulders, a broken nose and a tattoo on his chest that said something like "Make my day."

He has fallen to my M-1 as a marine in Korea to be boiled in a helmet with K rations. And he has been driven to me holding a borrowed Purdey, as delicate and lovely as a thoroughbred's front leg, while harvesting him in Wales. There he was served in a fifteenth-century mansion with a string quartet in an outer chamber.

When raised in captivity, pheasant beaks must be snipped or shrouded so the birds won't kill each other. Their spurs must also be removed. So remember this when sending a pup for a retrieve. Older dogs know how to handle this scrapping bird when it's merely crippled, but a pup can be ruined as a retriever for life with but one pugnacious encounter.

And though cock pheasants have a death wish for each other during mating season or when penned up, nevertheless the pheasant is a communal bird. Often you'll find flocks of thirty or more holed up in the same thicket.

There are essentially two ways to hunt this bird. A group of hunters can walk abreast through a row crop, driving the birds before them, to be encountered by blockers at the end of the field who are also armed. The birds are simply bottled up, and when they loft, they're shot (I wish it were that easy). Pheasant have a deep reluctance to leave cover, so any time you drive the bird before you, it is known he'll probably take flight at any edge.

Pheasant are also hunted by one or two men (or women) with a retriever who literally hunt the bird the way they'd go for bobwhite. Yet pheasants are not inclined to sit to point. Consequently, the best dog tactic is to have a retriever that chases the bird down, leaps and lofts him. Another equally good method is to put down a retriever on whistle and hand signals. Cast the dog out and around the bird's assumed position and work the dog back into the gun—once again trapping the bird.

This does not mean the bird can't be pinned down and kicked to flight. This happens often in great mounds of tumbleweeds where the birds hole up, thinking they are safe only to have you barge in—or your dog cast in—and the birds explode.

Pheasant fly only as a last consequence. Their preferred means of escape is by foot. You'll see them run before you like dust-covered, humpbacked ghosts: The back just naturally humps up. And they'll run so long as you move. But there's a trick. Especially in rattling row crops.

Just stop, don't make a sound. Sometimes the suspense gets too much for the bird and he'll either blunder into view or launch, giving you a shot.

Yet there is another hole card up the China bird's sleeve. That's his doubling back. You think you've got him bottled, you think he's being herded, and then up he comes—twenty yards behind you or far out to side. So you should have your phalanx of hunters walk in a sag, the point men being to front on either side. Then the bird must go back among you.

But you can foil him by dropping back yourself. Keep checking your back trail, look to see movement. Or every so often turn about and go backward, quartering as you do. Or call your retriever in and cast him behind the hunting party. You may find the fugitive.

And don't think some dogs can't outrun a flying pheasant. This bird is a relatively short-flight performer. He's not built for anything else. Up he goes, levels out, soars, gives a few beats in flight and glides to earth where he hits and runs. But a dog in pursuit will be on him soon if it's not a windy day, and the bird will be obliged to fly again. Well, a pheasant just doesn't have that many touch and gos in him. He'll sputter, flop and be brought to hand.

Targets of opportunity for the pheasant hunter—apart from row crops—are mounds of tumbleweeds, hedgerows, waterways (those ditches left to cover where fields are drained), creek banks, weeds around abandoned farm buildings and lake or marsh shores. Yet the most classic shot I ever made on a cock pheasant was from the first tee box at the Mulvane, Kansas, municipal golf course. Field Ch. Keg of Black Powder, Jim Culbertson's immortal field trial Lab (Jim's a retired physical education administrator from Wichita, Kansas) had run off to the left in the rough and launched the bird to fly straight across the fairway. It was a hole in one.

Pheasant dogs require special care afield. Pheasant love row crops, which means rich dirt that goes to dust when dry and disturbed. Plus, row crops are dust and pollen holders that when shook powder the dog's nose, eyes and mouth. Carry plenty of water if there are no puddles or creeks about. Water the dog often and groom him to remove debris, especially in the eyes. Pour water from your Thermos into the bottom outstretched eyelid and watch the debris bead. Then brush it away.

Stubble also rubs a dog's belly and scrotum (or teats) raw. Inspect the dog often and carry salve to deal with these sensitive areas.

Some hunters want their pheasant dog in rubber or leather boots, for busted-off stubble can be razor-sharp. The dog can hunt out the day, but come next morning he'll limp from his crate.

There's hardly a breed of gun dog I haven't taken to the pheasant field. They'll all do good. But a dog that can track is an asset. We're after a running quarry (incidentally, did you know "quarry" is an Old English term meaning entrails given to a dog as a treat for a job well done?). If the day's not too dry, the dust too heavy, the dog will follow the ground trail and eventually launch the bird. But eighty yards out does you little good. So the dog must be tractable to the whistle, he must leave off his forward drive when you ask him to—even if he's on the trail of hot scent.

And speaking of trailing, this can come up in a test hunt. Well, there's a way to train for it. Get a wing-bound duck and introduce it to heavy cover. Let your dog see the duck depart. Wait five minutes, then cast your dog. He will pick up the scent and trail. And why the duck? Well, they go without stopping—unlike an upland game bird. And they are wide-bodied, leaving lots of scent on the adjacent cover.

There'll come the day it snows, and that's when you and Pup should head for the pheasant fields. The birds leave visible track to start with and you can trail them. Plus they're not so willing to fly. If they get wet under the wings, they can easily freeze and die. (For this reason, don't ever forego hunting the bird in a cold rain. Pheasant hate water and do not want to move even in stubble, for they'll get wet.) Consequently, the pheasant will dig under the snow, thinking he's safe. That's when your retriever can have fun: sniffing out the bird's blow hole and diving in to either come up with bird in mouth or see the world explode as the pheasant comes squawking out.

But don't be surprised in your duck blind to hear a pheasant *car-ruuuuuuuunk* on the far side of the pond as he's flushed by some varmint and then later appears swimming through your decoys. If the pheasant had webbed feet (for he has an athlete's legs), he'd outswim a duck. But once in the water he can't launch. So let him make it to shore for a sporting chance.

Remember, too, there's something about pheasant that tantalizes a dog. Once the bird is in your hand, the dog will generally insist on leaping for it. So wear a vest or coat with game pouch where you can put the bird out of sight. This is especially important if you're hunting a young pup that wants to linger and not cast out for a new hunt.

Make sure your bird is dead before stowing it. I've been spurred good by a stunned bird I put in the game pouch that later came to life, rearing and kicking.

And know this. There is a fad making its way across America now and it's called "the pointing retriever." Now pointing retrievers, to my knowledge, are obtained by praying, not breeding. I've had some that would and many that wouldn't. But I can say this, if a retriever is going to point a bird, it'll usually be a hen pheasant. Okay? And as for a never-fail pointer of birds, I'll stick with the English Pointer and save my retrievers for displaying when getting birdy so I know when the game's coming up without having the dog go to point.

I've worked pheasants in game reserves, in the wild fields of several nations and even experienced the classic European drive shoot where the birds are lofted to you over a row of high trees. I've hunted the China bird hard and I've had thousands brought to hand on the retriever test circuits. But I've never regarded this bird as common. His flair, his grit, his flash and his wit have always caused my heart to skip a beat. The pheasant is truly king of the farm belt and he'll never forget it. Once you know him, neither will you.

14

Waterfowl

I'VE LIVED A LIFE like most people. I've had too many mistakes, too few victories, most goals never achieved, and I've not always treated my fellow man like I should have. But there was one thing I did do and I tuck the memory of it into my heart like a love token. I never missed a legal day of duck hunting for seven years. If we assume a legal season is 60 days, then that means I went duck hunting every morning for 420 straight days. Sure I had a job. I had to work. But I had some suburban acreage with a twenty-eight-acre pond on the back forty, and I could get from my bed to my blind—with my waders pulled over my pajamas—in five minutes.

Now it's like an old man once told me, "Carry a rock in your pocket for seven years and you're going to learn something about rocks." I learned the magic of entering nature and trying to hide and then dupe a wild creature—that knows all about the wild business and wild survival— to my lair. I learned how to make my own decoys and duck calls and how to blow them, and how to make a duck boat and train a retriever and plant wapato duck potato and Japanese millet so the ducks would be presented a Garden of Eden. I learned how to pour hot coffee over the edge of a tin cup so it wouldn't burn my lip, and how to stamp my feet and flail my arms to stay warm, and how to elevate my stand with shipping palettes when flood water raised the pond's level.

But the thing I learned most was what to expect and how to care for a duck dog. And to that knowledge we'll now turn.

THE DUCK DOG

First off, most duck dogs never see the bird fall. They are either forced back in a pit blind or pushed down behind cover or buried under a tarp in a skiff, or, let's face it, the old dog's asleep at your feet. And here they come! Four red-legged mallards ram a wedge past your stand and you fire . . . and your buddy fires . . . and the heavens roll over and the acrid white smoke billows past your head and the sound of heavy bodies hit the water. That's when Pup wakes up. And if he's young and full of juice he just runs right through the wood planks nailed to the blind. But if he's old he stands and stretches and looks up at you with fogged-over eyes, and you tell him to lay back down and you go get the ducks yourself.

So Pup must be in the prime of life. And be born and cultivated to water love. And be bred and fed to take cold water. For the most eager retriever living will hold back if he just doesn't have the coat and the constitution for cold water. You know this for a fact: You're the same way.

So Pup blunders out of the blind and starts looking for ducks, head high. If Pup knows his business he'll guess where all four birds are. He's launched for them from this blind before. And he'll know what way the wind's blowing and he'll know all about water currents . . . 'cause they'll carry his birds away so he must hurry.

And the first thing Pup will look for is the crippled duck. That's the duck that will escape by diving or will go to shore and hide in cover. So Pup ignores the dead ducks. Now here's where the handler and Pup must be in tune. The handler must be able to read his dog, to know what the dog knows, what the dog's thinking. If the handler reads in Pup's composure the fact that Pup knows where all the birds are and what to do, then the handler props his gun against the blind and relaxes.

If not, if the handler sees right off that Pup is confused, then he helps his dog. He whistles Pup down and gives him either an oral command or hand signal, or both. Or he'll cheer the dog on when he's going in the right direction and deny him if he's going off course. Or the handler may just be throwing a bunch of pebbles or spent shells to lead Pup on . . . like a carrot before a donkey. Or the guy may leave the blind and go direct Pup to the bird.

This is the classic flooded timber shoot of Stuttgart, Arkansas. Dog is placed on deer hunter's tree stand attached to tree. Gunner fires.

Dog leaps.

Dog is helped to make retrieve and get his seat back by handler thrusting down on the back of the dog's head to lift his body up.

If you don't have a tree stand, then put Pup on stump. Note how hunting Lab marks off upraised gun.

But this dog is not our Pup. Our Pup knows all about this duck hunting, for we taught him the business: taught him in yard training, and Happy Timing, and marking, and lining and all the custom features we put on him—just to please our particular bent.

The handler can also assist Pup by sluicing all crippled ducks down. That is, he shoots cripples on the water, thus relieving Pup, if possible, of a marathon swim. I've seen dogs gone for an hour. If the water is cold that's quite a challenge for a dog. Then, too, the handler helps Pup by not sky-busting flights. That is, he doesn't go for vapor-trail ducks. He shoots only those in his range and he shoots them dead.

Many duck dogs work from boats. Once again the dog seldom sees what's happening. And all the above rules apply. But there's something else. When Pup gets back with the duck, he can be helped into the boat by the handler getting the dog's elbows over the gunwale of the boat and then pressing down on the back of Pup's neck. This lifts Pup's rump and helps him climb into the boat.

Now, generally speaking, dogs that hunt in Dixie don't need to be schooled in handling ice floes or ice aprons, but those up north sure do. Many ducks land on ice next to the honey hole or along the shoreline, and Pup must climb up there to retrieve them. Which means Pup must contort himself like a shrimp, grasping with his front elbows, bending his rump completely under the ice floe and digging with his elevated back claws to edge upon the ice. Not ever dog can do it. And all dogs should be schooled in this technique of climbing aboard. Thoughtful trainers will bait a raft with dog food and force Pup to mount it from the water for a tidbit.

Remember, too, that Pup can more or less hear your voice and whistle commands when he's in swimming water, but when he's in running water, he's kicking up an awful lot of interference. Therefore, be sure to whistle him down in running water before giving a voice command. Otherwise he won't be able to hear you.

Something else a duck dog must do is deliver to hand. Work on this. A dog that lays its game on the bank to shake water can often be off again—chasing the game that just escaped because it was dropped. Insist on Pup holding the bird. Train on this.

It's also important when shooting in a public game area that Pup heel all the way to the blind. If he's off and about, the slob hunters who hunted the day or two before without a trained dog will have left your limit in cripples and dead ducks. And Pup will bring these to you, and there you are, sun's not up, you haven't popped a cap, but you've got a limit of ducks. Not only are you denied the pleasure of bagging your own

Ice chunks float on river as Pup is trained with dummy.   *Butch Goodwin*

game but—and this is important—you are subject to arrest by a federal or state game warden for having game in hand before legal shooting time.

Now there's a world of controversy about whether or not to leave a retriever outside a duck blind. I happen to know it helps the duck hunter—but, alas, many duck hunters think just the opposite. For centuries ducks have been brought to the decoy man's net by a moving dog. Prior to the invention of gunpowder, the waterfowler would have gone hungry without a dog. Now, though, waterfowlers fallaciously believe a moving dog will spook ducks. It won't—it will attract them—but arguing such can be a waste of breath.

Now I want to emphasize this: A good meat dog will break at gunshot. He wants to be off and away to get the jump on a strong cripple. But too many dogs break at the sound of the safety being clicked. As for me, who cares? I like the fire in a bright and birdy dog. But this can bother other hunters.

Therefore, if your dog is to be stationed outside the blind, he'll need to be rock steady. That is, if you don't want him going at the sound of the safety or the firing of the gun. If he's not steady, you'll have to stake and chain him.

THE DOG BOX

And in that regard let me introduce the dog box. Omar Driskill is high on this—he may even have been the first to develop it—and I need to explain what it is and how you use it.

Omar tells us, "It all started with an incident in a rice field pit over at Monroe, Louisiana. Normally dogs hunt waterfowl on the outside of the pit. You know those pits that are four by twelve feet, made of steel and sunk in the ground so they just clear the water. Well, this day the hunters didn't want the dog on the outside, so they decided to drag him in.

"You can imagine what goes through a dog's mind to be dragged into one of those dark holes and lie in the water at the feet of hunters. So the dogs always object. So you grab muscle and you grab hair and you wrestle the dog until you get him to break over and plop in.

"So these guys were pulling on that dog and he's just locking up and he's skidding, and when they finally overmuscled and overpowered him into the pit—he leaps. And when he leaped, he knocked over a gun, and the gun hit a crossbar, discharged, and they had to amputate the leg off an eighteen-year-old boy.

Photo shows construction of dog box with cutout for exit and entry, plus eyebolt.

Here the dog is extremely short-tied to eyebolt.

The alternatives to a sunken dog box is for Pup either to be buried in the pit blind or left out totally exposed to the weather and view of incoming waterfowl.

"Just terrible. For a boy to have to go through life with one leg just because some hunters couldn't get a dog in a pit. So I got to thinking, why put the dog in the pit in the first place?"

To that end Omar made a dog box of wood: the dimensions of the thing being thirty-six inches long, twenty-four inches high, nineteen inches wide and the top open or closed. Then he cut a U in the front for the dog's neck to set, plus he can easily leap out of the U, and in the bottom of the U is screwed in a big O-bolt to snap to a chain that leads to the dog's flat collar. And Omar wants a short chain—no more than four feet.

The box is buried outside the hunter's sunken pit, just deep enough so that the dog's head is even with a man's head who's standing in his own pit. For now the dog can see the same thing the man sees, plus he can learn to mark off the swing of the gun. But that's no more important than this fact: The dog now has his own sanctuary, his own place.

Omar explains, "I told you I wanted a short-tied dog. You know the average duck hunter, if he ties his dog up at all he'll do it with a twelve-foot rope, chain, what-have-you. Then the dog can roam around, he can go anywhere. Then when those shotguns go off, he leaps and runs and hits the end of that chain and he's flipped over and freaked out. But through the restraint of a four-foot chain, you can handle that dog and keep him from hurting himself. Plus he's not roaming about and getting in the way, over there trying to lick you in the face or take your sandwich from your mouth.

"Finally, it's important you have a dog box at home you can transport to the field and train the dog in. To me we train our dogs sort of like boot camp, but then opening day of duck hunting season is like Vietnam. It's the real thing. And nothing should change for the dog. He should be taken to the hunting field exactly like he was trained at home. Then he has no surprises."

Another benefit of the dog box, besides the dog marking down the gun, is his head is even with the hunter's head. That way the dog can look up and his dark face won't spook the ducks (my pink flesh will) and I will follow the dog's eyes. Those eyes will tell me exactly where the ducks are and when to take 'em.

SOMETHING TO SAY

Also, many birdy retrievers are vocal. That is, they whine on game. And when the dog's at my side, I can shush him. But if he's outside my presence, then quieting him can create too much disturbance.

Many duck hunters feel it is cruel to force a dog to sit in cold water all day—like hunting in flooded timber. You're hugging a tree and kicking a wader-clad foot to move the water and make the decoys look like they're feeding, but poor old Pup, all day long he's sitting in water halfway up his chest.

Well, I've never known a dog to mind sitting in cold water. But there's a limit. You get a day so cold that the dog comes back from a retrieve shaking grains of ice, and no way should he be sitting in water. You'll hear his teeth chatter, you'll see his muscles convulse. That's outside Pup's comfort range, though such a day won't kill him. It's heat that does dogs in, not cold weather.

So we carry a portable deer stand and attach it to a tree in the flooded timber—or we tell Pup to kennel up on a stump. That way he's out of the cold water except when working.

DECOYS

It's the responsibility of the duck hunter to short-tie his decoys. Some dogs panic when tangled in long strings. Others just drone along and all the cords are gathered and all the decoys bunched up and the dog pulls the raft to sea and releases them. Subsequently, incoming ducks decoy out there and that's the end of the hunt unless you get out and rearrange your set.

Now I've talked of formal decoy shooting. But many duck opportunities come from pond jumping or river sneaking. Crawling up a dam, peering over, finding the birds and working your way into ambush position is lots of fun. Still you'll need a retriever to fetch 'em up once you've shot. But you don't need him while shooting. This is when the duck dog must sit and stay where you leave him.

For if he moves, the floating ducks may lift for the water (they'll come back out of curiosity but that means a wait for the hunter). Or you may shout at Pup to stop and that'll lift the flight—never to come back. Now ducks can be lured to shore by a dog working a bank: appearing, then disappearing, over and over. The rafting ducks will paddle to him, their idea being, I guess, that what they can see won't hurt them. But when a dog first appears, the initial response of most wild flights is to launch. And the average pond jumper doesn't have time to wait for the birds to return.

So you need a dog with a handle on him. Yet he must also have great spirit when asked to work.

At an early age pups must be introduced to decoys on dry land.

The truly great duck dogs also know when it's permitted to touch land and when it's forbidden. And if they don't know the difference, they at least honor the whistle and hand signal and do as bidded. For many shot ducks will fly from water and go to land. I've had them soar a mile away and the dog was stopped at the top of a far hill and given a *driving* "Back" to propel him whatever distance awaited him before he found the bird.

Good duck dogs also mark down deadfall while they're retrieving. Sure, the ducks come in while the dog's in the decoys: They show not the least concern about him. And now Pup's looking for an old bird and new ones are falling all about him. Never mind. He stays with his initial hunt, for we taught him on a mowed-grass field never to switch birds.

But, alas, there is one calamity in duck hunting that seems impossible to avoid. Dogs work so close to a gun in the blind that they can suffer noise-induced hearing loss. I've had more than one old warrior that was stone-deaf. But you don't need to be. For your own sake, wear ear protectors.

And on those sunny "bluebird" days when the ducks don't fly, or the days of fog when any sane duck would be walking, you can sit in the blind and sip your coffee and rub Pup's ears and tell him how much you love him. You don't need ducks to go duck hunting.

15

Popcorn Quail

ANY MAN who spends a great part of his life studying quail is a birdbrain. Should he do this sighting down the sickle tail, between the cocked ears and over the long nose of a retriever, then it stands to reason this man's a birdbrain who's gone to the dogs.

Such is me.

I've learned, for example, that a dog locates 90 percent of all quail within twenty-five feet of an edge. Having been raised this way since a juvenile peep, the quail grown to maturity will winter this way. Their range changes between the two seasons but always incorporates an edge, be it tree, ditch, fence, wall, creek, railroad, path, a piece of abandoned farm equipment, what-have-you.

Consequently, a man who wants to get his retriever into quail will cast him to mixed cover, to linear and upright objectives.

A quail's nature is to eat early and late, loaf in between, roost at night and dust all day. So quail are not to be found anywhere they can't readily get their feet on the ground. Sure, they'll bed down on grass, but that grass must be close to loose soil, such as a plowed field.

In nesting season momma-quail wants to get her peeps to food fast and keep them dry in passage. She fears wet feathers en route as much as a feral cat at her nest. One menace can do peeps in just as readily as the other. Peeps die from exposure to moisture.

Momma-quail is quite similar to momma-human. She wants her

home next door to the shopping center. Momma-human would rather take a beating than haul her brood downtown. She wants to get in and out fast, avoid the hassle, limit the exposure to danger and fatigue.

Momma-human's suburban shopping center is a great expanse of concrete. She doesn't walk through tall, wet grass to enter the supermarket.

Same with momma-quail. Her shopping center is an expanse of bare soil, with domed cover and sparse vegetation. The soil is bare, not matted with grass. An ideal example would be a stand of bicolor lespedeza or a thicket of multiflora rose. Momma-quail wants the earth to dust, to keep her brood dry and to more readily peck at and pick up seed that's shattering and falling from the canopy above. She doesn't want to scratch in the grass to find a meal.

It stands to reason as the peep is raised, so shall the juvenile and adult behave. Consequently, it's a purposeless bird hunter who stalks a matted grassland back for quail, or a sea of sedge grass, or a pasture of Bermuda.

Down in Dixie, ancestral home of the bobwhite, it's said, "When that sun comes out in the afternoon, you can't lift a bird with a bulldozer."

Bird dogs are sniffers, not coursers; they hunt by scent not sight. In the afternoons when the sun shines bright, quail hole up. They lounge in loafing spots and take it easy, lower their metabolism.

When you're downwind from a farmhand sweating in a high sun, you get a whiff of him more readily and more distinctly than should you chance upon him lying by the creek bank, lazying in the shade. A body at rest just puts out less scent.

One reason is the lungs breathe more shallow. And that's one scent retrievers seek in hunting quail: bird breath. And if retrievers don't home in on bird breath, then tell me how all of them can tell the difference between a live bird that's fully breathing, a crippled bird that's partially breathing and a dead bird that's not breathing at·all? They do, you know. You bet your prized shotgun they do.

Also, when you dizzy a bird and tuck his head under a wing and plant him (I never went into this with you, for a dizzied bird is too hard to control and predict), why does the dog have a more difficult time scenting him than when the bird's just shackled and his head is coverless? What other answer but the bird's breath?

If you want Pup to fetch deadfall quail, you'll have to teach him: It's a case of scent discrimination brought about by repetition and association.

Suffice to say, when a bird is out hustling, he's giving off scent a

Wade Culbertson (son of author's longtime quail/Lab hunting companion, Jim Culbertson of Wichita, Kansas) takes quail from Pup's mouth. Note dense cover being hunted.

dog's programmed to smell: breath and body scent. When that bird is injured or killed, or at rest, the breath scent diminishes and, possibly, the body scent is altered.

A retriever smells only on the intake, never on the outgo. Watch one when his radiator's boiling over: the bellows of his rib cage stroking 300 times a minute, tongue hanging, mouth frothed. The dog's taking shallow gasps at a rate of approximately five per second. What do you do when you want to smell something? Walk into the kitchen, chili's on the stove, cake's in the oven. You stop before the stove and take a deep breath. You change locations and take another deep breath before the oven.

That's how Pup should breathe while hunting, taking no more than one great, deep breath per second.

Birds emit a scent cone. Liken it to a woman's fan. The fan can be short or long, it can be spread open or closed. As encountered in the field, the scent cone may fan out 90 degrees or be folded nearly shut. The fan may be 100 feet long or six inches.

Let's say the birds are holed up: emitting little scent, shallow breathing. Pup comes huffing through. The bird's scent cone is two feet wide. Pup's panting, gasping for air, and bounds "breathlessly" through. He's scented no birds.

If Pup were clean-bored and deep breathing, running cool, able to concentrate on what he's scenting instead of getting his breath, he'd snatch a bit of bird scent in passing—get enough of it for his olfactory senses to register the find. He'd have you into birds.

To do that Pup must be running cool. A cold day will help, but even then you need to augment Pup's cooling system. This is done through preseason conditioning, exercising Pup most every day, expanding his lungs, building up his endurance.

Also, you can help keep Pup running cool by releasing him to field five minutes, then calling him for a drink of water, letting him run another few minutes, then heeling him for a second drink.

Other things affecting bird scent are vegetation and type of soil. It's a fine-bored pooch that can smell a bird in early-morning alfalfa, for example.

Also, when earth is loosely packed, such as sand, dogs will have more trouble scenting than when they confront birds on clay-based or hard-packed earth. If it's raining this also cuts down on scenting. In the rain a dog has to come right up on the bird to handle it. Yet if you have damp grass, this is good for dog work if you've also got some breeze. But no breeze, no birds. Then should that breeze turn into a real strong wind, this will diffuse bird scent. Not only smother it but scatter it about. You'll always find dogs have a difficult time handling birds in a high wind.

It may have been an oddity when Jim Culbertson and I started hunting quail with our Labs. We'd put four to eight boondock journeymen down and flat vacuum a field. We'd have to call the dogs off for conservation—leave something for seed.

RETRIEVERS AND QUAIL

Nothing is more fun for hunter and dog than hunting bobwhite with retrievers. You know when the bird's coming up by reading the dog. He'll tell you everything that's happening before him, and inside him. The cock of his ears, the beat of his tail, the stiffness of his haunches, the bow of his neck. They all scream out this is it, the birds are coming up.

I guess there's nothing that'll birdy a retriever up like a bobwhite quail hunt. They flat love it. And they'll go all day. They love the blur and the scat and the clapping surprise of the rising birds. They love their scent. And their cover, where they live in cool, dark places. And there's intersecting streams where the dogs plop belly down and laugh up at you with foxy faces.

Only one real problem. I once had a young Lab named Thunder who had such a full-bored nose and was so quick he continually brought live quail to my hand. I'd just release them, but Thunder would be crestfallen. His head would drop, his tail would drop, he'd slowly slouch away. So I began holding his live retrieves, and praising him, until he ran away, and then I'd release the live bird to the wild.

Don't pass up quail hunting with your retrievers. It just might be the most fun afield you and Pup will ever have.

16

The Hunting Retriever Clubs

THE HUNTING RETRIEVER CLUBS have to be the most exciting thing that ever happened to the American bird hunter and his retriever. For not until now has there been the opportunity where a hunter and his retriever could go to train, to learn, to develop and to crown their joint efforts by the dog becoming a bona fide hunter and even a hunting retriever champion.

This is what thousands of duck and upland game hunters have wanted for years. A no-nonsense, true-to-life, sure 'nuf successful training and testing program where bird hunters meet, train, learn together, sponsor clinics, help each other and test their dogs afield: not looking for retrievers to perform meaningless tricks, but rather to get the bird in hand. And to do so by using humane, thoughtful, guaranteed dog training techniques to create the finished hunting retriever.

The hunting retriever clubs grew out of the duck-jammed flyways and bayous of Louisiana, where duck and bird hunting are taken about as seriously as a heart attack. Where going for feather has been raised to a science and hunting retrievers has become an obsession.

Since the days of Audubon, Louisiana has led the nation in bird hunting. Little wonder that a practical and humane hunting retriever training program would develop there. What's startling though is how

American sportspeople could be so lucky to get such a bonus handed them. For these Louisiana hunters to share their secrets, their shortcuts and their successes, the retriever fans of America must have been doing something right.

No matter what the developmental stage of your retriever, there's a stake in the hunting retriever program in which to handle him. There are events for started dogs, intermediate dogs and finished dogs. There are test hunts in each category. And surprisingly, some of the points earned in either of the beginning categories can sometimes be applied toward a hunting retriever championship.

This is truly a hunting retriever program conceived by hunters, perfected by hunters and put on by hunters. Hunters who know what you as a fellow hunter—and your dog as a hunting retriever—need, and they deliver it to you!

This is the opportunity of a lifetime for each of us who love bird hunting and trained hunting retrievers to get together, to grow together and to accomplish together. Where dog and hunter and bird will be the joint beneficiaries. The man or woman, in having the satisfaction of going afield with a dog he or she has trained, and to successfully meet nature on its own terms. The dog, in doing what God put him here to do—and doing it well! And the bird populations of America, in being conserved: For a bird down will be a bird in hand.

As I said in Chapter 4, there are three different national hunting retriever clubs in America now. I'll not go into detail as to how they are all the same and yet they all differ. These clubs are not that old, and everything is still in a stage of flux. Rules change yearly; events are being constantly altered.

But I leave you with this one caution. I saw the classic retriever field-trial circuit self-destruct because it adapted tests that demanded a dog trip over his own instincts in order to place. And to train a dog to deny his own nature too often required brutality on the part of the trainer.

Don't let this happen to the new hunting retriever test format. There really is only one criterion: That is, each test must duplicate some part of a day's hunt afield. Nothing else matters. That's the sum and the total of it. If the test could be a natural part of a day's hunt, then include it, if not, then deny it—and anyone who supports it.

Remember, the hunting tests are where you and Pup go for both your benefits. And there or in the field the rule must be: Happy Hunting!

Appendix:

First Aid for Water Dogs

MY CHOICE for America's premier, general-practice vet is Dr. Dick Royse of Wichita, Kansas. We've worked together now for thirty years and I've yet to find him wrong. My experience has been that he can diagnose a dog over the phone better than most vets can with the animal right before them on the table. Albeit, someone's got to be reliable and observant in presenting the symptoms.

Only six months younger than I, the two of us were born in the same Depression-era world and grew up with the same experiences and philosophy. Doc got through school by hard work, not by brilliance. He became an excellent practitioner by devoting his life to it, not by some divine gift of surplus smarts. Royse works hard, thinks deep, regards the dog's plight more important than the profit and loss statement and identifies personally with every dog he brings along. Dogs are not just his patients, they are his friends. And he feels a commitment never to let a friend down.

I contacted Dick Royse a year ago and told him I wanted something unique for this book. "Let's get together an article," I told him, "for water dog first aid. It's never been done before, it's needed, and you're just the man to do it."

Doc accepted the assignment and together we produced what follows.

Sprains

It's a Thursday afternoon, Doc's clinic is closed and he's in his office, tinkering with a smoking pipe carved with eight sides to the bowl. He spends a lot of time getting the thing stoked, rears back in his spring chair and says, "I think water dogs may be a little more vulnerable to sprains and muscle pulls than other sporting dogs. When that seventy-pound dog hits the water in a pond with a mud bottom four to six inches deep, he is powerful and he is moving. And I think that is something that probably he may be vulnerable to. So after a shoot, a water dog is more apt to come up with a sore leg or something like that.

"The remedy? Just rest him. You probably won't need to see a vet unless he can't work. But more than likely, the dog is so birdy he will want to go hunting the next day, limping or not. Let him—if he can walk. I don't see how he could hurt himself. He'll be protecting the affected limb. He'll care for himself."

Puncture Wounds and Lacerations

"Water dogs may be a little more vulnerable to puncture wounds depending on areas where you might be hunting. A lot of broken glass is scattered in our ponds along with pieces of barbed wire, tin cans, old trot lines and more junk. You don't know what's been thrown in there.

"You treat a puncture wound much the same way as you do a laceration but with one exception I'll mention later. With lacerations we're into soft-tissue wound management. And nowadays we throw away our antiseptics, our peroxides, our distilled water . . . instead, we use saline.

"Saline is an isotonic solution. In other words, it has the same constituency as body fluids. And you can get it from your veterinarian in 150- or 250-cc bottles. And that is what you clean a wound with. And I mean that's the first thing you use and the only thing you use.

"Now if the dog is bleeding, that must be stopped. Place a saline-soaked three-by-three gauze pack on the wound and apply pressure. Hold tight until the bleeding stops. When that occurs, you can stay afield if you want—should you be after upland game. But if you're after waterfowl or geese or shorebirds, then you've got to be careful.

"Why? Because the wound is going to stay wet. So what to do? For upland hunting, stop the bleeding and apply a gauze pack. Remove the compress, flush the wound with saline and apply a bandage. But don't cover your gauze with tape, we need air to get to the wound. Secure the gauze by catching adjacent hair with tape and just catching the ends of the bandage.

"But what if the bleeding won't stop? Then you need, and only as a last resort, to apply a tourniquet. I swear, maybe more dogs have been hurt by a tourniquet than have been helped. You must be so careful. Remember to only apply the tourniquet tight enough to impede bleeding: no more! And remember, too, a tourniquet should be loosened every fifteen minutes for about five minutes. Then repeat the sequence until Pup gets to a vet. First aid has failed, you must now have the skills of a professional, or second aid.

"Remember this about bandages. Always use gauze packs, never cotton. The fibers in cotton stick to the wound. And remove the bandage as soon as you can, for air is beneficial in wound healing. And never apply a bandage so tight it becomes a tourniquet.

"Now know this. On a large-area wound treat only with saline, never with distilled water or antiseptic. Antiseptics can inhibit healing because they destroy good bacteria as well as the bad. Your dog needs the good bacteria to heal all right. And stay away from powders. Too often they use talc as the vehicle to carry the medicine, but talcum inhibits healing.

"So now let's return to puncture wounds—and you're after waterfowl. Well, the difference between a laceration and puncture wound is that with the latter you may have something stuck in the dog. Try to get the thing out if it will come easily, but never use force. The only exception I could think of would be porcupine quills: With them force is a necessity. Once the foreign object is removed, then you treat the wound just like a ordinary laceration. But there are a couple of cautions. Puncture wounds must heal from the inside out. So the more the wound can bleed, the more it self-cleans. This is an instance where you promote bleeding rather than impede it. If the puncture wound is small in opening but deep, this means the foreign object carried infection in, and now the depth and small size of the hole seals that infection shut.

"This is especially true between toes of a water dog. That webbing is a great place for infection to go crazy. But let's say you've let the wound bleed out and want to stay hunting. Well, a gauze bandage will do no good: It will stay wet. So ask your vet for some pliable, rubberized material, such as Co-Flex or Vet-Wrap. This is excellent to protect a sore foot with, for it is waterproof and it molds to the foot.

"Now puncture wounds must heal from the inside out. Which means on wound maintenance you must keep the outer part of the wound open, and this is hard for many dog owners to do. They've got a gaping hole, let's say, it's bloody, it looks sore. And they pity the dog, only to let the outer skin heal and now the infection is trapped deep in the wound. So you must keep the puncture wound open and draining and keep applying whatever antibiotics the vet gives you deeply into the wound.

"For a puncture wound on an upland game hunt, an ordinary gauze pack bandage will suffice." Doc removes the pipe from between his teeth and says outright, "I'd say every puncture wound, by necessity, requires the treatment of a vet. The dog can be infected with a gas-producing bacteria, or gangrene, from a puncture wound. He can die. So no matter how minor the puncture wound looks to you, eventually get to the vet."

Poisons and Toxic Exposures

"I checked with the Kansas Game and Fish Commission," says Doc, "on what they use these days for fish kills and algae. I'm not saying this will apply to the whole country, but to some of it, I'm sure. And what they're using for fish kills is rotenone. The guy said the parts per million are so minute they have never had trouble with livestock or anything. And for algae they are using copper sulfate and they are using chelated compounds. And he said there again that has never caused any problems because it's applied in such a diluted portion. So he said he could think of nothing they are using nowadays that would pose a hazard to a water dog.

"Now if you're hunting in an area close to a large feedlot, then feedlot runoff could have a lot of contaminants in it. For instance, leptospirosis. That's passed in the urine of cattle. Cattle are vaccinated for it, so it's pretty well under control. But if you should happen to be hunting on the downside of a large feedlot, and you get a dog that comes up sick, it might be valuable information to know. With a sick dog, just get him to a vet."

Eye Injuries

"Eye injuries might be a little more common for a water dog because they're charging through the cattails and reeds. They've got their eye on the bird and they're not seeing anything else. So they can get a stabbing-type poke in the eye. It's difficult to evaluate eye injuries because they're usually more serious than they appear. You should do nothing more than flush the eye with common boric acid eye wash—if you do this much—and head for a vet.

"In case seeds settle in Pup's eyes . . . you'll see it . . . walk a dog through a dusty, milo field and pull out that lower lid and pour boric acid in there, and the junk will just form a chain you can brush from the side of the nose. Don't forget to do this. Oh, you can use common water, but it can be irritating. Boric acid is better. Also, your vet can supply you an eye lubricant that makes the eye tear excessively, constantly washing out foreign matter. Many hunters wouldn't be without it."

Ear Problems

"Now I see quite a few water dogs around here, a lot of Labs, and I don't see a lot of ear problems that I would say were caused by water in the ear. But if you have a dog that has a history of ear problems and some of them are kind of chronic, in other words, you get the ears cleared up for six months and they are okay and then they flare up again, then water could be an aggravating factor. Should you have such a water dog, you should ask your vet for a good petrolatum-based ear ointment that will repel water, and squirt the ears a short time before you go hunting. I'm talking about a petroleum-based product, something with grease in it as a protective agent."

Seizures

"If you've got a dog that is prone to hypoglycemic seizures or epileptic seizures, you want to use caution. A dog that a suffers seizure in the water can be in serious trouble. If you dog is hypoglycemic, you want to be sure it eats a candy bar, or gets Karo syrup an hour before you go hunting. With epilepsy you've just got a problem that can't be helped. Be ready to go to sea should the dog lose control."

Hypothermia

"I've had people ask me about hypothermia and the cold weather on a duck hunt. I really question whether a healthy dog is going to become hypothermic. There must be unbelievable conditions and prolonged exposures for that to happen. Or the dog has developed some kind of illness or stress that you don't know about. But as far as hypothermia, I just don't see it. When a hunter sees his dog shivering, he thinks, Oh boy, that dog is cold. All the dog is doing is warming himself. That's how he's creating energy with those muscles. It's like rubbing two sticks together."

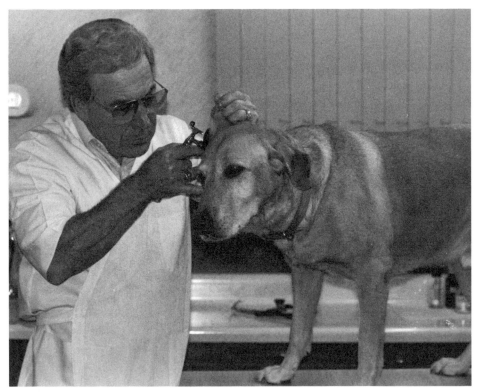

Dr. Dick Royse inspects Lab's ears: Seldom is water in the ear a problem for a water dog.

Choking

"If I had a water dog that inadvertently got choked, and he comes out of the water and snorts around and coughs and coughs and then is okay, I wouldn't worry about it. But if he inadvertently aspirated some water into his lungs, he probably is not going to quit coughing. And he's going to have a moist, hoarse cough that will go on. He will run a little ways and stop and cough, over and over. If that happens, I would get the dog to a vet. He has fluid in the lungs. And this can create secondary pneumonia. So the first thing I would do as a vet would be to get this dog on some diuretics, which will suck the fluid out of the body cavity. Then I'd put him on antibiotics.

"So far as drowning I just can't see it, unless the dog gets physically hung up in coiled wire, barbed wire, something like that."

Algae Poisoning

"Now during the summer you train these water dogs in algae-skimmed ponds. I don't think I have ever seen a case of algae poisoning. I've seen those dogs come in that I think may have drank out of a dirty, old, algae-contaminated pond or some packing-plant canal . . . and the worst thing that I've ever seen come out of that is an upset stomach and bowel. I just don't think I've ever seen a true poisoning. I used to hear about that, but I don't even see it mentioned in the literature any more. Just be sure you keep your dog current on all vaccinations."

Lyme Disease

"We now know Lyme disease has transferred from the deer tick to two or three other species of tick. If that ends up in the common, old, brown dog tick, then we'll have problems all over the country. There is a vaccine available I'd sure recommend for any field dog.

"As for the tick—what the general public doesn't know to look for is a tiny, tiny thing. And be a little fussy about taking these ticks off. Be sure you don't have any nicks or cuts on your hands. You'll catch the disease from the tick. So wash your hands well after going over the dog."

I interrupt Doc, saying, "How do you get 'em off? I've always left the head."

Doc laughs and says, "Getting the head, I think, is a myth. And I've never seen any problem in leaving it. Here's what will happen. The head will simply shrivel up, the dog's body will form a little red spot and a scab, and when the scab comes off, everything comes off with it.

"What you do is grasp the tick with your thumb and forefinger as close to the skin as you can, grip hard and then pull the tick out and put some antiseptic on the hole."

Fractures

"If you suspect fracture, take everything easy. Keep Pup quiet. Otherwise he will aggravate the injury. Do not attempt to manipulate the injured limb or feel about the torso, neck or head.

"Under no circumstances should you try to apply a splint. You run a good chance of lacerating muscle tissue or severing an artery or vein with razor-sharp bone splinters.

"If you suspect a spinal injury, slide Pup on a flat surface to be used as a stretcher and head for professional care. And don't assume Pup's without fracture just because he's walking or running. If you suspect fracture, treat for shock and head for the vet."

Shock

"Shock is always our primary concern. It may occur with any serious injury. Symptoms are a docile Pup, depressed, semiconscious or unconscious, possibly rapid panting and a fixed stare to the eye.

"Wrap Pup in a blanket and keep him warm and quiet. In most cases of shock, a dog experiences a rapid drop in body heat. This must be brought back to normal fast.

"Approach Pup from behind and toss a blanket over him. He'll possibly partially self-wrap himself and you can finish bundling. The blanket will warm Pup, plus assist in immobilization.

"Generally, if Pup's hurt bad enough to go into shock, he'll probably need a vet's care."

Heat Stroke

"With heat stroke you see rapid, heavy panting or raspy breathing with acute oxygen deprivation. Another indication is if Pup collapses.

"You must lower Pup's body temperature and do it fast. Even dump him in a cold stream. Remember, Pup's belly is comparable to a human's wrists. That's where the largest supply of superficial blood vessels lie closest to the skin. This is where you concentrate a coolant. Should you have ice in a chest, wrap some in a cloth and apply to the base of Pup's skull. Or carry a bag of Kwik-Kold, the instant ice pack that's activated by striking the bag of white granules.

"If Pup can drink, give small amounts of ice-cold water at frequent intervals. Too much water, however, and Pup may vomit.

"You've got to work fast with heat stroke. Pup's normal body temperature is 101.5. Heat stroke can send this temperature soaring. When body temperature rises, it causes tremendous congestion, which impedes circulation to the brain. This creates undue pressure, which, in turn, may damage brain cells. That's why we apply ice to the base of Pup's skull."

Poisons

"Symptoms ordinarily take two forms: 1) incoordination, extensive nervousness to the point of seizure and convulsion; and 2) profuse vomiting and/or diarrhea. Unfortunately, with some poisons, and this is the bad part for the dog corpsman, you see no symptoms at all.

"We used to say anytime a dog was thought to have ingested poison, we would recommend prompting the dog to vomit. But now we know should that poison be acid or caustic, we do not induce vomiting. The reason for this is that caustics and acids can damage the esophagus and stomach to the point where vomiting might cause hemorrhage. Should you want to induce vomiting, this can be accomplished by giving one tablespoon of peroxide orally. Lacking this, place one teaspoon of salt on the rear of Pup's tongue. Save the vomitus and give to the vet for analysis.

"Also, if Pup goes into seizure or convulsion, you must protect him from self-injury. Wrap him in a blanket."

Accidental Gunshot

"The distance Pup was shot will determine the amount of injury. This will indicate how much shock to expect and how deep the pellets penetrated. If you accidentally shoot Pup close enough to knock him down, you're going to be dealing with a tremendous amount of shock. So back to the blanket. Wrap Pup, keep him warm and get medical help as fast as you can.

"But let's say you just sprinkle Pup so he yipes, there's only a few blood specks. You're probably not going to have any immediate problems. Cleanse the shot holes with saline and either keep on hunting or head for a vet. It's up to you.

"But if Pup's hit hard, and he comes through shock, he's going to be so muscle-sore he can hardly walk. This can be expected with any dog shot from a distance of forty yards or less."

Spider Bite

"These things are hard to detect in the field. Yet anywhere from three to seven days later, Pup can likely show an area of dead tissue between the size of a dime and a quarter. The area will turn black, infect, and fall out. Don't attempt home treatment. Get Pup to a vet."

Snake Bite

"First off, you ignore the dog and kill the snake. We must determine if it's of a venomous species. If you can't find the snake, then look at the bite. Nonvenomous bites generally have a U-configuration and are multitoothed. Such bites appear as superficial scratches and cause little pain. Cleanse well with saline and seek further treatment.

"However, a venomous snake usually leaves two fang marks. And the victim may exhibit instantaneous, severe pain in the bite area. Depending on the potency of the venom, the dog may become incoordinate, vomit, convulse or go into coma. If you don't get the dog to a vet within four hours, the outlook for recovery is poor.

"There's little you can do in the field for a venomous snake bite. Get the snake. Keep the dog quiet. Permit no exercise that will stimulate the venom's flow. Don't cut and suck: That went out with the stagecoach.

"Contain the venom by applying a flat, constricting band between the bite and heart. Impede the flow of venom, but don't block off arterial circulation. You're not applying a tourniquet. Plus, if the bite is high enough on the leg, put a second constricting band beneath it. Keep the venom away from the paw. We are, in fact, isolating the venom in the area of the bite. The reason? Venom isolated in the paw by just one constricting band can cause damage resulting in amputation.

"Now a constricting band (or bands) is properly adjusted if a finger can be inserted with but slight force. The band should be left intact until definite treatment is provided or a minimum of two hours.

"Let's look at a typical scenario. You're miles from any metropolitan area. Your dog is bitten. You take the dog to a rural vet for treatment, but that vet's a large-animal doctor. He can treat Pup, but he doesn't stock antivenin. But you do. That's right, you carry antivenin so the vet can give it to Pup.

"Medical science is constantly improving antivenin. Present shelf life is twelve to eighteen months. That's under refrigeration. Yet your car can get mighty hot. So carry antivenin in a plastic bag within your ice chest. When not afield, refrigerate antivenin and buy a new kit often. Your vet will advise you.

"And, yes, once again you'll need to treat Pup for shock. Get him wrapped in a blanket.

"One final thing, whether or not you apply ice to Pup's snake bite is up to you and your vet. It has been noticed, however, that the iced appendages of humans suffering venomous snake bites result in more amputations than for patients who don't use ice."

Bee Sting

"If Pup is stung by a flight of honeybees or a bumblebee, make a baking-soda paste and pile it on a half-inch thick to the affected area. Cover with a damp compress and hold for fifteen minutes. Follow this with an ice pack. The same treatment applies for wasp stings."

Burns

"For localized burns, apply ice, snow or your handkerchief saturated with water from a winter stream. A large-area burn will cause shock. Now you've got to make a decision on priorities. Should you cool the wound or get the dog wrapped in a blanket? Large burns trigger Pup's body to consume great amounts of liquids. If Pup is not immobilized, he will aggravate dehydration. Make your decision and proceed fast.

"Incidentally, never apply ointment to a burn. That's just something the vet has to remove so he can proceed with treatment."

Choking

"If there's something lodged in Pup's throat and you can handle his jaws so you don't get bitten, then open his mouth and pull the tongue out as far as possible. Now, can Pup inhale air? If he can't, pick him up by his hind legs, hanging him head down, and give him a sharp slap either high across the back of his shoulders or across the front of his chest.

"If a small object's lodged in the trachea, it may jar out, or you may stimulate coughing, which can blow it free. Remember, never stick your fingers down Pup's throat. He may reflex-bite and/or you might lodge the object even deeper.

"To pull Pup's tongue from his mouth, compress the hinge of the jaw to force the mouth open, then continue to squeeze your thumb and forefinger on opposite sides of Pup's jaws, pressing the flesh of Pup's cheeks beneath his teeth. Now you can reach the tongue. Once the tongue's pulled out and slid to side, Pup can't bite."

Foreign Object in Ear

"You may remove anything from Pup's ear you can reach with your fingers. But if there's anything in the ear deep enough to cause discomfort, you probably won't be able to see it. Get to a vet."

Electrocution

"Drag Pup from whatever shocked him with a loop made of leash, belt or check cord—anything not wet and not a natural conductor. You may be confronted with three simultaneous emergencies: respiratory failure, shock and burns. Induce breathing by artificial respiration. Lay Pup on his side, legs extended, and place one or both hands flat in the middle of Pup's rib cage three inches behind his shoulder. Press firmly, listen to air expire and release abruptly. Repeat sequence twenty times a minute.

"If Pup has stopped breathing, you've got five minutes to get him started. After that time irreversible brain damage may already have occurred.

"Also, Pup has been shocked; he's in shock, so you must treat for shock.

"And you may well have to treat for burns."

Dogfight

"Injuries resulting from a dogfight can include broken bones, pulled teeth, dislodged eyeballs, punctures and lacerations. Be prepared to treat for shock. A dogfight can be a total calamity. Avoid fights at all costs.

"Dousing fighting dogs with water sometimes gets them separated. But the surefire method is for two men, each grabbing a dog by his hind legs, to pull the dogs apart and swing each dog in great circles.

"Now heed this advice. If your dog's been in a fight and all you see is a couple of little puncture wounds and blood spotting, don't dismiss it as a minor wound. Puncture wounds can come back to haunt you. When a dog opens his mouth and bites, he makes a puncture wound with his upper jaw plus a puncture wound with his lower jaw. When he closes his mouth—this is a big, strong dog—he tears the tissue from top to bottom where he's biting. The result? The dog bite has loosened all that skin from wound to wound, and four to five days later you'll get a big abscess there.

"So get your bitten dog to the vet as soon as possible to get the puncture wounds flushed out and to have the dog put on antibiotics."

First-Aid Kit

In our first-aid kit are gauze bandage rolls, two- to four-inch width; adhesive roll, two-inch width; three-by-three-inch gauze packs; tourniquet of your choice; blanket; Kwik-Kold instant ice pack; saline; boric acid eye wash; snake antivenin; baking soda; old sweat sock (for over foot); salt or hydrogen peroxide; eye lubricant; rubber boots and our waterproof adhesive. We've mentioned other items you may also include. It depends on your expected needs.

The kit can be arranged in a toolbox, the cutaway bottom of a bleach bottle with a plastic film cover secured by a rubber band, a small fishing tackle box, a discarded briefcase or almost anything else you have around the house.

Should you be using your water dog for upland game, then there are two other items you need. A pair of bolt cutters to cut Pup out of a wire fence should he get hung up while leaping, and a set of toenail clippers in case Pup splits or throws a nail.

Before and after season you should have a general physical for your hunting dog. See that he's fit to start. See that he's endured the rigors of the hunt and come out all right. Also, during the off season it's your responsibility to keep Pup in shape by Happy Timing him, road working him in sled dog harness or taking him on long walks. You want Pup fit for the first day. That can only be achieved by summer conditioning.

In every instance rely on your vet. He's your friend, he's your dog's friend and he can make the difference between a sad hunting season and a stellar one. Don't skimp on vet fees, they are the greatest investment you and Pup can make.

X